Paris
Apartments

Paris
Apartments

 teNeues

Editor:	Haike Falkenberg
Editorial coordination:	Ana G. Cañizares
Texts:	Francesca Torre, Cristina Montes, Ana G. Cañizares, Paco Asensio, Mihail Moldoveanu
Art director:	Mireia Casanovas Soley
Layout:	Pilar Cano
German translation:	Inken Wolthaus, Lars Oscenda
French translation:	Michel Ficerai
English translation:	Matthew Clarke, Ana G. Cañizares
Spanish translation:	Marta Casado Lorenzo, Sol Kliczkowski
Copyediting:	Ana López

Published in the US and Canada by
teNeues Publishing Company
16 West 22nd Street, New York, N.Y. 10010, USA
Tel.: 001-212-627-9090, Fax: 001-212-627-9511

Published in Germany, Austria and Switzerland by
teNeues Verlag GmbH + Co. KG
Am Selder 37, 47906 Kempen, Germany
Tel.: 0049-(0)2152-916-0, Fax: 0049-(0)2152-916-111

Published in the UK and Ireland by
teNeues Publishing UK Ltd.
Aldwych House, 71/91 Aldwych
London WC2B 4HN, UK

www.teneues.com

ISBN: 3-8238-5571-9

Editorial project: © 2002 **LOFT** Publications

Domènech, 9 2-2
08012 Barcelona, Spain
Tel.: 0034 93 218 30 99
Fax: 0034 93 237 00 60

e-mail: loft@loftpublications.com
www.loftpublications.com

Printed by: Gràfiques Ibèria S.A, Barcelona, Spain

April 2002

Die Deutsche Bibliothek – CIP-Einheitsaufnahme
Ein Titeldatensatz für diese Publikation ist bei
der Deutschen Bibliothek erhältlich.

The Parisian lifestyle
dedicated to privacy,
intellect, gastronomy,
conversation, individualism,
good taste and "*savoir vivre*"
is reflected in each and
every project in one way
or another.

Paris, France. The City of Light, La Grande Nation... this dynamic metropolis has been coined once and over again, never failing to conjure up notions of grandeur, romanticism and elegance. For 800 years it has been the undisputed hub of a country whose long history and deeply rooted nationalism have enriched its culture and doted it with a particularity recognized by the rest of the world.

The unique past and character of Paris has created a cultural blend that becomes evident in its architecturally rich landscape. The twentieth century brought with it the wave of modernity, an international movement which the French took in stride –the capital city's range of traditional retrospection, radical innovation and tentative progression generated a mixture of courage and defiance that for the last two decades has produced an incomparable diversity in architecture and design. Remaining ever-loyal to its classical buildings and monuments of centuries past, there is constant evidence of new and original structures that have been ingeniously inserted without jarring the splendor of 19th century Paris. This duo of defiance and acceptance has moulded Paris into the fascinating and complex city that it is, owning the greatest and most varied wealth of contemporary buildings.

This peculiar Parisian style has naturally translated into the homes that lie behind those buildings, both old and new. Architects and interior designers concoct spaces filled with stunning contrasts that effortlessly coexist and play off of one another. Their creations often lead to eclectic homes that breathe extravagance and vigor, while others remain far more minimalist yet always with that elegance and attention to detail so particular to Parisian interiors.

PARIS APARTMENTS is a breath-taking collection of interior spaces like these, featuring interior architects and decorators like Masakasu Bokura, Marie-France de Saint-Félix, and Andrée Putman. Inspired by spectacular views of the charismatic city, their concepts materialize into spacious attics, small studios, and loft-like spaces that appear in a variety of styles anywhere from minimalist and elegant, to modern and classical, to wild and eclectic. This mixture of styles is the key feature which characterizes most Parisian homes. In many of them reside artists, actors, chefs, writers and the designers themselves. The Parisian lifestyle dedicated to privacy, intellect, gastronomy, conversation, individualism, good taste and "savoir vivre" is reflected in each and every project in one way or another. The city's richness in architecture and design –which embraces that of yesterday, today and doubtless tomorrow– reflects these values held so closely by those who live there, in a very "modern" place that encompasses all its states of beings and epochs.

Der Pariser Lebensstil, der
Intimität, Intellekt,
Gastronomie, Unterhaltung,
Individualismus und gutem
Geschmack einen ersten Platz
einräumt, wird auf die eine
oder andere Weise in jedem
der Projekte reflektiert.

Paris, Frankreich. Die Lichterstadt, Die Große Nation... Diese dynamische Metropole, die immer wieder umgemünzt wurde und niemals aufgehört hat, die Symbole von Größe, Romantik und Eleganz zu verkörpern. 800 Jahre hindurch war sie der unbestreitbare Mittelpunkt eines Landes, dessen lange Geschichte und tief verwurzeltes Nationalgefühl ihre Kultur bereicherte und sie für die ganze Welt zu etwas Besonderem machte.

Ihre einzigartige Vergangenheit und ihr individueller Charakter haben ein kulturelles Miteinander geschaffen, das sich in einer vielfältigen architektonischen Landschaft wiederspiegelt. Das 20. Jahrhundert brachte einen Modernisierungsschwung mit sich, eine internationale Bewegung, die die Franzosen von Anfang an unterstützten. Die Kombination traditioneller Geschichte, radikaler Modernisierung und schwankenden Fortschritts in der Hauptstadt schufen eine Mischung aus Mut und Herausforderung, die während der letzten Jahrzehnte eine unvergleichliche Vielfalt in Architektur und Design entstehen ließ. Obwohl den klassischen Gebäuden und Denkmälern vergangener Zeiten weiterhin die Treue gehalten wurde, machten sich unaufhaltsam neue und originelle Strukturen breit, die harmonisch integriert werden, ohne die prächtigen Gebäude des 19. Jahrhunderts zu stören. Diese Dualität von Herausforderung und Anerkennung hat Paris seine Form gegeben und es zu einer komplexen Stadt mit den meisten und verschiedenartigsten modernen Gebäuden gemacht.

Dieser besondere Pariser Stil hat offensichtlich weder vor den alten noch den neuen Wohnungen dieser Gebäude Halt gemacht. Die Architekten und Innenarchitekten erschaffen Räume überraschender Gegensätze, die mühelos miteinander harmonieren. Ihre Werke zeigen oft eklektische Wohnungen voller Extravaganz und Kraft, aber auch minimalistische Einrichtungen, in denen jedoch immer die Eleganz und die Liebe zum Detail - so typisch für den Pariser Wohnstil - gewahrt bleiben.

PARIS APARTMENTS stellt eine eindruckvolle Zusammenstellung dieser Wohnungen vor, bei der namhafte Architekten und Innenarchitekten wie Masakasu Bokura, Marie-France de Saint-Félix oder Andrée Putman mitgewirkt haben, die sich alle von den spektakulären Ausblicken auf diese charismatische Stadt der Künstler, Schauspieler, Küchenchefs und der Designer selbst inspirieren ließen. Der Pariser Lebensstil, der Intimität, Intellekt, Gastronomie, Unterhaltung, Individualismus und gutem Geschmack einen ersten Platz einräumt, wird auf die eine oder andere Weise in jedem der Projekte reflektiert. Der Vergangenheit, Gegenwart und zweifellos auch die Zukunft umfassende architektonische Reichtum spiegelt diese Werte seiner Bewohner in modernen Räumen wieder, unabhängig von Epochen oder Gesinnungen.

La vie parisienne, faite
d'intimité, d'intellectualisme,
de gastronomie, de
conversation, d'individualité,
de bon goût et de *"savoir vivre"*,
est toute entière dans chacun
des projets, sous un aspect
ou un autre.

Paris, France. La Ville Lumière, La Grande Nation… cette métropole dynamique sans cesse réinventée a toujours su évoquer la grandeur, le romantisme et l'élégance. Pendant 800 ans, elle fut le cœur incontesté d'un pays dont l'histoire et le nationalisme profond ont enrichi la culture, lui conférant un particularisme reconnu dans l'ensemble du monde.

La personnalité et le passé uniques de Paris ont créé un creuset culturel qui devient manifeste dans la richesse architecturale de son décor. La vague de modernité du vingtième siècle, dans son élan international, fut acceptée avec sérénité par les Français. La gamme de tradition rétrospective, d'innovation radicale et d'avancée timide de la capitale a généré un mélange de courage et de méfiance engendrant une incomparable diversité d'architecture et de design au cours des deux dernières décennies. Demeurée loyale à ses immeubles et monuments classiques des siècles passés, elle a constamment accueilli des structures nouvelles et originales, s'insérant avec esprit et harmonie dans la splendeur du Paris du XIXéme. Ce mariage de méfiance et d'acceptation a façonné Paris en une cité complexe et fascinante, arborant le plus important et divers trésor d'architecture actuel.

Le style parisien si particulier s'est naturellement traduit dans les demeures cachées derrière ces façades, d'hier et d'aujourd'hui. Architectes et décorateurs d'intérieur ont fait naître des espaces nourris de contrastes saisissants qui coexistent sans effort et interagissent librement. Leurs créations mènent parfois à des lieux éclectiques respirant l'extravagance et l'énergie, d'autres demeurant bien plus minimalistes sans oublier l'élégance et le souci du détail propres aux intérieurs parisiens.

PARIS APARTMENTS est une collection captivante de ces espaces intérieurs, figurant des architectes et décorateurs d'intérieur comme Masakasu Bokura, Marie-France de Saint-Félix et Andrée Putman. Inspirés par les vues spectaculaires de la cité charismatique, leurs concepts prennent vie dans de spacieux attiques, de petits studios et des lofts parcourant tous les styles du minimalisme élégant au classique moderne, en passant par les folies d'éclectisme. Ce mélange de styles constitue le trait principal caractérisant la plupart des demeures parisiennes, qui abritent, pour nombre d'entre elles, des artistes, acteurs, chefs, écrivains et les créateurs eux-mêmes. La vie parisienne, faite d'intimité, d'intellectualisme, de gastronomie, de conversation, d'individualité, de bon goût et de "savoir vivre", est toute entière dans chacun des projets, sous un aspect ou un autre. La richesse de l'architecture et du design de Paris – embrassant aujourd'hui entre hier et demain – reflète ces valeurs chéries par ses habitants, dans un environnement " moderne " accueillant tous les états d'esprit et les époques.

El estilo de vida parisiense dedicado a la privacidad, el intelecto, la gastronomía, la conversación, el individualismo, el buen gusto y el *savoir vivre* se refleja en cada uno de los proyectos de una u otra forma.

París, Francia. La Ciudad de la Luz, La Grande Nation... Esta dinámica metrópolis se ha reinventado una y otra vez, sin dejar nunca de evocar los principios de grandeza, romanticismo y elegancia. Durante 800 años ha sido el eje indiscutible de un país cuya larga historia y arraigado nacionalismo han enriquecido su cultura y la han dotado de una singularidad reconocida en todo el mundo.

El pasado único y el carácter de París han creado una mezcla cultural que se hace evidente en su rico paisaje arquitectónico. El siglo XX trajo consigo una ola de modernidad, un movimiento internacional que los franceses secundaron desde el principio. La combinación en la capital de la retrospección tradicional, una innovación radical y un progreso vacilante generaron una mezcla de coraje y desafío que durante los dos últimos decenios ha producido una incomparable diversidad en la arquitectura y el diseño. Manteniéndose leal a sus edificios clásicos y monumentos de épocas pasadas, hay numerosos testimonios de estructuras nuevas y originales que han sido incorporadas ingeniosamente sin desentonar entre los esplendorosos edificios del siglo XIX. Esta dualidad, desafío y aceptación, ha modelado París, convirtiéndola en una ciudad cautivadora y compleja, que acoge el más variado y mayor número de edificios contemporáneos.

Este peculiar estilo parisiense se ha trasladado, evidentemente, a los hogares que estos edificios albergan, tanto antiguos como nuevos. Los arquitectos e interioristas crean espacios llenos de sorprendentes contrastes que conviven sin esfuerzo. Sus creaciones a menudo conforman hogares eclécticos que respiran extravagancia y fuerza, mientras que otros son mucho más minimalistas, aunque siempre conservan la elegancia y gusto por el detalle tan particular de los interiores parisienses.

PARIS APARTMENTS es una imponente recopilación de estos interiores, que incluye la obra de arquitectos y decoradores como Andrée Putman, Masakasu Bokura o Marie-France de Saint-Félix. Inspirados en las espectaculares vistas de esta carismática ciudad, sus conceptos se materializan en espaciosos áticos, reducidos estudios y lofts que muestran una amplia variedad de estilos, desde el minimalista y elegante hasta el moderno y clásico, pasando por el lujoso y ecléctico. Esta mezcla de estilos es la clave de la peculiaridad que caracteriza a la mayoría de los hogares parisienses. En muchos de ellos viven artistas, actores, chefs, escritores y los mismos diseñadores. El estilo de vida parisiense dedicado a la privacidad, el intelecto, la gastronomía, la conversación, el individualismo, el buen gusto y el "savoir vivre" se refleja en cada uno de los proyectos de una u otra forma. La riqueza de la ciudad tanto en arquitectura como en diseño, que engloba el pasado, el presente y, sin duda, el futuro, refleja estos valores a los que tanto se aferran sus habitantes, en un espacio moderno que abarca cualquier carácter o época.

Location: Neuilly
Architect: Damien Brambilla
Photos: © Olivier Hallot
dbrambilla@orange.fr

In Neuilly

Being an exquisite chef, the owner of this apartment placed a great deal of importance on the kitchen, which he wanted to be open to the living room. The solution chosen by the architect was to erect a free-standing wall that reached neither the ceiling nor the walls of the kitchen area. Without dividing the living room in two, it creates distinct spaces and gives the impression of an extended living area. A window communicates the kitchen –consisting of stainless matte steel, glass, and a red counter– with the living/dining room, facing a window that opens out over the Bois de Boulogne. The living room displays stainless steel, red furniture, and tinted concrete. In the bathroom, concrete and slate are complemented by the delicacy of the teak wood, fiberglass and white ceramic.

Der Eigentümer, ein exquisiter Gourmet, legte großen Wert auf die zum Wohnzimmer hin offene Küche. Der Architekt fand eine Lösung mit einer freistehenden, küchenseitig errichteten Wand. Ohne das Wohnzimmer zu teilen, werden Räume geschaffen und der Eindruck einer Erweiterung der Wohnfläche erweckt. Eine fensterähnliche Durchreiche verbindet Küche und Wohnzimmer mit Blick auf den Bois de Boulogne. Im Wohnzimmer wird mit glattem matten Edelstahl, roten Flecken und gefärbtem Beton gespielt. Im Bad ergänzen Beton und Schiefer die Zartheit des Teakholzes, der Glasfaser und der weißen Keramik.

In Neuilly
Damien Brambilla

Le propriétaire étant un fin gourmet il attachait une grande importance à la cuisine qu'il souhaitait ouverte sur le salon. La solution préconisée par l'architecte a été une paroi libre, dégagée du murs et du plafond, aménagée côté cuisine. Sans scinder le séjour en deux, elle ménage des suspenses et donne l'impression que l'espace continu au delà. Un passe plat comme une fenêtre donne d'un côté sur l'inox brossé, le verre armé et la crédence rouge tomate du plan de travail, et de l'autre côté sur une vraie fenêtre de salon qui s'ouvre sur le bois de Boulogne. On retrouve l'inox brossé lisse, des tomettes rouges et du béton teinté dans le salon. Dans la salle de bain le béton et l'ardoise côtoient la délicatesse du teck, des pâtes de verre et de la cèramique blanche.

Al ser un exquisito gourmet, el propietario concedía mucha importancia a la cocina, que debía quedar abierta al salón. La solución del arquitecto consistió en una pared que no llega al techo ni a los muros, en la zona de la cocina. Sin dividir el estar en dos, organiza los espacios y da la impresión de que se prolonga más allá. Un pasaplatos a modo de ventana comunica la cocina y el salón, con su ventana con vistas al Bois de Boulogne. Encontramos acero inoxidable mate, mobiliario en rojo y hormigón teñido en el salón. En el baño el hormigón y la pizarra se complementan con la delicadeza de la teca, la libra de vidrio y la cerámica blanca.

Location: 13ème Arrondissement
Architect: Guilhem Roustan
Photos: © Patrick Müller
guilhem.roustan@free.fr

Avenue de Choisy

The small dimensions of this apartment, located on the top floor of a building, do not prevent it from offering all the luxuries of a modern lifestyle. The square space is divided into several areas, which are organized to form a single continuous space. The refurbishment undertaken by Guilhem Roustan included a small extension in the form of a terrace, connected to the interior by means of glass walls. These not only make the interior spaces look considerably larger but also open them up to abundant natural light. Economy of means, decorative sobriety and a design strategy designed to highlight the home's main attraction – the views. These are the ruling elements of this apartment and they explain the absence of any superfluous elements.

Trotz der reduzierten Maße dieses Apartments in der obersten Etage, sind alle Voraussetzungen einer modernen Wohnung gegeben. Auf einer viereckigen Fläche sind die verschiedenen Bereiche auf einem einzigen, durchgängigen Raum untergebracht. Anlässlich der Renovierung erweiterte Guilhem Roustan die Wohnung um eine teils innen- teils außenliegende und durch verglaste Trennwände verbundene Terrasse, die den Raum optisch vergrößern und gleichzeitig Tageslicht einfallen lassen. Sparsame Mittel, dekorative Nüchternheit und das Fehlen überflüssiger Elemente zusammen mit dem herrlichen Panoramablick machen den Charme der Wohnung aus.

Avenue de Choisy
Guilhem Roustan

De dimensions réduites, ce dernier étage dispose des avantages d'une maison contemporaine. Un niveau carré accueille les aires en un espace unique, continu et d'une certaine netteté visuelle. La rénovation de l'architecte Guilhem Roustan, a inclus une extension en terrasse diluant les frontières extérieur/intérieur et faisant se rencontrer et communiquer les deux espaces par des baies vitrées. Elles élargissent visuellement l'espace et diffusent la lumière naturelle. Économie de moyens, sobriété décorative et stratégie intérieure soulignent les points clés du lieu. Régie par les vues le définissant, ce lieu est argumenté par l'éradication des éléments superflus.

Las reducidas dimensiones de este apartamento, ubicado en el último piso del edificio, no le impiden disponer de todas las prestaciones de una vivienda actual. Una planta cuadrada acoge las diferentes áreas, organizadas en un único espacio continuo. La rehabilitación de la casa, a cargo de Guilhem Roustan, incluyó una pequeña ampliación en forma de terraza, comunicada con el interior mediante paredes acristaladas, que además de ampliar visualmente el espacio, permita la entrada de luz natural. Economía de medios, sobriedad decorativa y estrategia interior dan protagonismo a lo mejor de la vivienda: las vistas. Ellas son el elemento que define esta casa y determina ausencia de elementos superfluos.

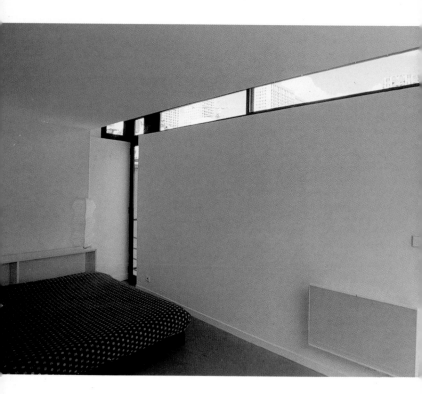

Location: 11ème Arrondissement
Architect: Pier Luigi Copat
Photos: © Michel Denance
copat@club-internet.fr

Rue St. Maur

This apartment, tucked into a garret, may be small but it still manages to fulfill all its domestic obligations. Unnecessary partitions have been eliminated to create a fluid, well-communicated space flooded with light. The walls have been painted a pristine white to take full advantage of the luminosity, and the structure of the wooden beams has been left exposed to evoke an atmosphere similar to the industrial lofts that have become so fashionable lately. Pier Luigi Copat is the architect responsible for this project, and his guiding principle for the decoration and fitting-out of this apartment was simply to achieve the maximum functionality in a space that was refurbished on a very low budget.

Alle häuslichen Funktionen sind auf dem reduzierten Raum dieser Dachwohnung untergebracht. Unnötige Zwischenwände wurden entfernt, um einen offenen, fließenden und ineinander übergehenden Raum zu schaffen. Die Wände wurden in reinstem Weiß gestrichen, um die Helligkeit zu intensivieren, und die Holzbalken blieben sichtbar, um die Atmosphäre der in letzter Zeit zur Mode gewordenen typischen industriellen Lofts zu vermitteln. Das Leitmotiv des Architekten und Projektverantwortlichen Pier Luigo Copat für Dekoration und Ausstattung ist maximale Funktionalität in einem mit minimalen Mitteln zurückgewonnenen Raum zu erreichen.

Rue St. Maur
Pier Luigi Copat

Ce petit appartement accueille toutes les fonctions domestiques, profitant des combles de l'immeuble l'abritant. Les cloisons inutiles ont été éliminées pour créer un espace diaphane, fluide et bien communiqué. Les murs sont blanc immaculé pour optimiser la luminosité et les poutres en bois apparentes pour créer une ambiance similaire à celles des lofts industriels, dans l'air du temps. Il en résulte un refuge où prévaut l'absence d'éléments superflus. L'architecte Pier Luigi Copat est responsable du projet, avec pour critère de décoration et d'équipement une fonctionnalité maximale pour un espace récupéré, avec un minimum de ressources.

Todas las funciones domésticas están contenidas en este reducido apartamento que aprovecha el espacio abuhardillado de un edificio. Se han eliminado tabiques innecesarios para lograr un espacio diáfano, fluido y bien comunicado, las paredes se han pintado de blanco inmaculado y para conseguir mayor luminosidad y se ha conservado a la vista la estructura de vigas de madera a fin de conformar un ambiente semejante al de los típicos lofts industriales tan de moda últimamente. El responsable del proyecto es el arquitecto Pier Luigi Copat y el criterio de decoración y equipamiento de este apartamento no es otro que el de conseguir con los mínimos recursos la máxima funcionalidad de un espacio recuperado.

Location: 11ème Arrondissement
Architect: Pier Luigi Copat
Photos: © Olivier Hallot
copat@club-internet.fr

Palette of Color

The top floor of this quiet building leads to a universe of clarity. Clarity of lines that vigorously run through the space; clarity of volumes that assume a weightless quality underneath a network of wooden beams; clarity accentuated by the enveloping presence of white walls. A unity of materials and colors also exists in the design. The shelves and doors conceived by the architect have been made from ash tree wood tinted in red. The shelves adapt to the form afforded by the slanted ceilings in the attic bedrooms, in this way using all available space so that circulation and fluidity is assured within the apartment. In the living room, the steel and polished concrete fireplace incorporates a glass wall at its right that permits a view of the fire on the way to the bedrooms.

Im obersten Stockwerk eines ruhigen Gebäudes gelangt man in eine Welt voll Klarheit. Klare Linien die kraftvoll den Raum durchkreuzen, fast schwerelose Elemente unter einem Geflecht aus Dachbalken, betonte Helligkeit durch die Allgegenwärtigkeit der weißen Wände. Materialien und Farben harmonieren. Parkettboden zieht sich durch die gesamte Wohnung. Die von den Architekten entworfenen Regale und Türen sind aus rot angestrichener Esche. Die Regale sind in ihrer Form der Dachschräge angepasst und lassen Raum zur freien Bewegung. Der Kamin aus Stahl und poliertem Beton im Wohnzimmer hat auf der rechten Seite eine Glaswand, wodurch man das Feuer auch von anderen Zimmern aus sehen kann.

Palette of Color
Pier Luigi Copat

Le dernier étage de cet immeuble paisible donne accès à un univers de clarté. Clarté des lignes découpées avec vigueur dans l'espace. Clarté des volumes presque aériens organisés sous les poutres apparentes. Clarté accentuée par l'omniprésence des murs blancs. Unité appréciable de tons et de matériaux. Les étagères et les portes de l'architecte sont en frêne teinté de rouge. La forme des étagères suit le toit, fluidifiant et libérant la circulation dans l'espace. Au salon, la cheminée en acier et béton sablé comporte une paroi vitrée à droite pour contempler le feu en se dirigeant vers les chambres.

En el último piso de un edificio tranquilo se accede a un universo de claridad. Claridad de líneas que se recortan con vigor en el espacio, claridad de volúmenes casi aéreos que se organizan bajo una bonita estructura de vigas, claridad acentuada por la omnipresencia de las paredes blancas. Asimismo se aprecia una unidad de materias y de colores. Las estanterías y las puertas concebidas por el arquitecto han sido realizadas en fresno teñido de rojo. La forma de las estanterías se adapta a la inclinación de la cubierta, dejando libre el espacio para la circulación. En el salón, la chimenea de acero y hormigón pulido tiene una pared de vidrio a su derecha que permite ver el fuego cuando se circula hacia las habitaciones.

Location: 6ème Arrondissement
Architect: Bruno Décaris
Photos: © Mihail Moldoveanu

Vernacular in Style

This apartment, adjacent to the Odéon Theater, is situated high up on a distinguished building and was completely refurbished by the architect. Inspired by the breathtaking views, Bruno Décaris decided to create two openings between the beams which appear as a great bay that opens out onto the city. He also emphasized the beautifully restored wooden structure. The apartment effectively concentrates all its functions in one single and spectacular space. Visual impact is assured in equal measures by the amazing vistas, the solid proportions and the structural design. The remaining visible interventions are minimal in order to promote comfort without disturbing the style of the space or over-charging the delicate balance between the panoramic views and the vernacular character of the construction.

Dieses Apartment in der Nähe des Odeon-Theaters liegt unter dem Dach eines von dem Architekten Bruno Décaris vollkommen restaurierten bekannten Gebäudes. In diesem Apartment sind in wirklich spektakulärer Weise alle Funktionen (Wohn- und Esszimmer, Küche) auf einen einzigen Raum konzentriert: Ausblicke, Proportionen und Strukturdesign gewährleisten die Harmonie. Die restlichen sichtbaren Interventionen wurden auf ein Minimum reduziert, um den erforderlichen Komfort ohne Beeinträchtigung der Atmosphäre zu gestatten und ohne das delikate Gleichgewicht zwischen dem Panoramablick und dem lokalen Baucharakter zu stören.

Vernacular in Style
Bruno Décaris

Voisin du théâtre de l'Odéon, cet appartement des combles d'un immeuble classé a été rénové par Bruno Décaris. Charmé par les vues sur Saint Sulpice, les Invalides et la Tour Eiffel, l'architecte a créé par des ouvertures entre les poutres une véritable fenêtre sur la ville. Parallèlement, la mise en valeur d'une charpente dûment restaurée a permis de concentrer la plupart des fonctions (séjour, repas, cuisine) en un spectaculaire espace unique : la théâtralité naît de la vue, des proportions et de la conception de la charpente. Les autres interventions visibles se réduisent au minimum : permettre le confort sans peser sur l'ambiance ou le délicat équilibre entre le panorama et le caractère vernaculaire du lieu.

Este apartamento, situado en lo alto de un distinguido edificio cercano al Teatro Odeón, ha sido restaurado por el arquitecto Bruno Décaris. Subrayado por las vistas, Décaris decidió crear, mediante aberturas entre las vigas, ventanas que se abren a la ciudad. El apartamento concentra la mayoría de las funciones (salón, comedor, cocina) en un solo espacio de gran espectacularidad: la dramaturgia está asegurada en igual medida por las vistas, las proporciones y el diseño de la estructura. Las otras intervenciones visibles están reducidas al mínimo, a fin de permitir todo el confort sin perturbar el aspecto del espacio, sin sobrecargar el delicado equilibrio entre la vista panorámica y el carácter vernáculo de la construcción.

Location: 6ème Arrondissement
Architect: Karin Léopold and François Fauconnet
Photos: © Vincent Leroux

Light and Dark

This old apartment, located in a traditional residential building, consisted of a small subdivided and poorly distributed attic. The inclined ceiling, typical of these kinds of Parisian spaces, incorporated large windows with splendid views of the city and the Eiffel Tower. The reform consisted in recuperating the valuable elements of the interior and liberating the surface area into one single 30 m² space. Walls and false ceilings were eliminated, exposing the wooden beams and achieving a greater ceiling height. The solution exhibited in this apartment features a closet that contains the toilet, heating, shelves and the front door. The extremeties of the closet house the shower, parted by translucent glass, and the kitchen.

Dieses alte Apartment in einem traditionellen Mehrfamilienhaus war eine kleine, unterteilte und schlecht genutzte Dachwohnung. Das Dach zeigte eine starke, für diese Pariser Wohnungen typische Neigung, und die Fenster gaben einen großartigen Blick auf die Stadt und den Eiffelturm frei. Durch Abriss von Wänden und Zwischendecken wurden die Balken wieder freigelegt und Höhe für die Gestaltung eines einzigen Raumes von 30 m² gewonnen. Die Lösung ergab ein Schrank, in dem Toilette, Heizung, Regale und Eingangstür Platz fanden. An den Schrankenden befinden sich die durch eine transparente Glastür abgetrennte Dusche und die Küche.

Light and Dark
Karin Léopold and François Fauconnet

Cet ancien appartement, situé dans un traditionnel immeuble d'habitation, consistait en un petit grenier divisé et mal utilisé. Le toit affichait une pente prononcée, propre à ce type d'espace parisien, et des fenêtres aux vues splendides sur la Tour Eiffel. La rénovation a porté sur la récupération des éléments précieux et la libération d'un espace unique de 30 m². Murs et parois furent abattus pour révéler les poutres et le dégagement en hauteur. Le projet se complète par une armoire accueillant toilettes, chauffage, étagères et porte d'entrée. La douche, séparée par un verre translucide, et la cuisine se trouvent aux extrémités de l'armoire.

Este antiguo apartamento, ubicado en un edificio tradicional de viviendas, era un pequeño ático subdividido y desaprovechado. La cubierta presentaba una inclinación pronunciada, propia de este tipo de espacios parisienses, y ventanas con espléndidas vistas a la ciudad y la torre Eiffel. La reforma consistió en recuperar los elementos valiosos del interior y liberar el espacio en un solo ambiente de 30 m². Se derribaron paredes y falsos techos para dejar las vigas a la vista y conseguir altura. El proyecto se resuelve con un armario que contiene el inodoro, la calefacción, las estanterías y la puerta de entrada. En los extremos del armario se encuentra la ducha, separada por un cristal translúcido, y la cocina.

Location: 6ème Arrondissement
Architect: Littow Architects
Photos: © Pekka Littow
littow@magic.fr

Rue de Savoie

The renovation takes place in the fourth and fifth floor of a 17th century building. A completely modern and simplistic approach was taken in creating a living space for its young tenants. Through the use of wood on virtually all surfaces, this material becomes the visual backdrop. The kitchen is also finished in wood panelling and integrated into the living area which comprises three contemporary sofas with interchangeable pieces. A rectangular black fireplace, framed against a white wall, is the only intervention on the far side of the living area. The bathroom features a cylindrical sink platform and translucent glass panels, while the bedroom contains a futon that lies under two narrow skylights.

Dieses Apartment in der 4. und 5. Etage eines Gebäudes aus dem 17. Jahrhundert wurde in ganz modernem und einfachen Design für seine jungen Eigentümer renoviert. Als Schwerpunkt der Dekoration wurde Holz für praktisch das gesamte Mobiliar gewählt. Selbst die in das Wohnzimmer integrierte Küche ist mit Holzpaneelen verkleidet. Ein schwarzer, rechteckiger Kamin, eingerahmt von einer makellos weißen Wand, verkörpert die einzige Unterbrechung im entfernteren Teil des Wohnzimmers. Dazu ein Bad mit zylindrischem Waschbecken und Paneelen aus durchscheinendem Glas sowie ein Schlafzimmer mit Futon direkt unter zwei schmalen Oberfenstern.

Rue de Savoie
Littow Architects

Cette rénovation s'intègre dans un appartement au 4° et au 5° d'un immeuble XVIIème. Le parti fut pris d'un design très moderne et simple pour le lieu de vie de ses jeunes propriétaires. Le bois, utilisé pour presque tout le mobilier, est l'élément clé de la décoration. Même la cuisine, intégrée à un salon de trois sofas contemporains, est en panneaux de bois. Une cheminée rectangulaire noire contre un mur immaculé constitue la seule intervention sur la partie la plus éloignée du salon. Le bain est dessiné par une plate-forme cylindrique et des panneaux en verre translucide. La chambre comporte un futon juste sous deux étroites claires-voies.

Esta remodelación pertenece a un apartamento situado en los pisos 4 y 5 de un edificio del siglo XVII. Se optó por un diseño moderno y simple para conseguir un espacio habitable por sus jóvenes propietarios. La madera se convierte en elemento clave de la decoración. Incluso la cocina, que se integra en un salón con tres sofás contemporáneos, está acabada en paneles de madera. Una chimenea rectangular de color negro, junto a una pared inmaculada, representa la única intervención en la parte más alejada del salón. El baño lo conforman una plataforma cilíndrica y unos paneles de cristal translúcido. El dormitorio consta de un futon situado justo debajo de dos estrechas claraboyas.

Location: 6ème Arrondissement
Architect: Ira Waldron
Photos: © Mihail Moldoveanu

Saint-Germain des Près

This studio/living space in the center of Saint-Germain is special for the relationship between its contemporary, sober and functional studio space, and the rest of the area dedicated to living which is marked by the vernacular charm of its medieval Parisian construction. These venerable walls, admirably restored, confer a certain nobility to the space, which nevertheless remains decidedly modern. Ira Waldron, the artist in charge of the project, is not very fond of doors which reflects itself in the fluidity between areas like the studio, dining room, kitchen and guest room. A narrow staircase leads to the bedroom and a sumptuous bathroom. Ira is also the creator of some of the furniture pieces seen here.

Diese Studio-Wohnung mitten in Saint-Germain überrascht durch die Verbindung zwischen dem modernen, nüchternen und funktionellen Studio und den anderen Räumen, die geprägt sind von dem "lokalen" Charme der mittelalterlichen Pariser Bauten. Die Eigentümerin des Apartments, eine Künstlerin, die hier mit ihrem Mann lebt, ist keine große Freundin von Türen; daher das Ineinanderfließen der verschiedenen Flächen von Studio, Esszimmer, Küche oder Gästezimmer. Eine schmale Treppe führt zum Schlafzimmer, von dem aus es in ein luxuriöses Bad geht. Einige der herumstehenden Möbel sind ebenfalls eine Kreation von Ira.

Saint-Germain des Près
Ira Waldron

Au cœur de Saint-Germain, cet atelier/demeure surprend par le mariage de la nef constituant l'atelier, sobre, fonctionnelle et contemporaine et des autres pièces, sous le charme vernaculaire du bâti médiéval parisien. Grâce à une restauration admirable, ces murs vénérables offrent une certaine noblesse à un ensemble pourtant moderne. La créatrice Ira Waldon, vivant ici avec son mari, a souhaité oublier les portes créant une fluidité remarquable entre les espaces : de l'atelier au séjour, en passant par la cuisine, la salle à manger ou la chambre d'hôtes. Un escalier étroit mène à la chambre et aboutit à une somptueuse salle de bains. Ira est aussi la créatrice d'une partie du mobilier animant la demeure.

Este taller-vivienda situado en pleno Saint-Germain sorprende por la asociación entre la nave de factura "contemporánea" y funcional que constituye el taller, por un lado, y el resto de los espacios, muy marcados por el encanto "vernáculo" de la construcción medieval parisiense, por otro. Estas venerables paredes, admirablemente restauradas, confirma una cierta nobleza al ambiente. A la artista propietaria de este apartamento, que vive aquí con su marido, no le gustan mucho las puertas, por lo que existe una importante fluidez entre los diferentes espacios, que corresponden al taller, al comedor, a la cocina o a la habitación de invitados. Una estrecha escalera conduce al dormitorio, con un suntuoso baño. Ira es también la creadora de algunos de los muebles.

Location: 14ème Arrondissement
Architect: Littow Architects
Photos: © Jacques Vasseur
littow@magic.fr

Studio Rue Liancourt

This tiny 24 m² studio fitted out for a Finnish couple demonstrates a clever and practical distribution of space. The small dimensions of the space called for a division of areas through the use of levels and materials. On one side, near the entrance, the kitchen receives light from the windows above the counter. On the other, a rectangular table serves as a working desk or a dining table. Above it a wall shelf was incorporated to hold books and decorative objects. A raised wooden platform next to this contains the mattress and integrated bathroom pod. A shower, toilet and basin are subtly and attractively concealed behind its translucent glass doors.

Dieses 24 m² Studio wurde für ein Pärchen entworfen und zeigt intelligente und praktische Ideen in der Aufteilung. Aufgrund der geringen Ausmaße wurde die Wohnung durch den Einsatz von verschiedenen Materialien und Ebenen gegliedert. Auf der einen Seite, nahe dem Eingang, befindet sich die Küche, die durch über dem Arbeitstisch gelegene Fenster Tageslicht bekommt. Auf der anderen Seite steht ein rechteckiger Tisch, der sowohl zum Arbeiten als auch zum Essen genutzt wird. Über diesem hängt ein Regal für Bücher und andere dekorative Gegenstände. Bett und Bad sind in ein Holzpodest eingelassen, wobei sich Dusche, WC und Waschbecken hinter durchscheinenden Glastüren befinden.

Studio Rue Liancourt
Littow Architects

Ce petit studio de 24 m², aménagé pour un couple, présente des idées de distribution intelligentes et pratiques. Les dimensions réduites réclamaient une division des espaces par des matériaux et des niveaux. Près de l'entrée, la cuisine est illuminée par des fenêtres au-dessus du plan de travail. De l'autre côté, une table rectangulaire tient le rôle de salle à manger. Elle accueille une étagère de livres et d'éléments décoratifs. Une plate-forme en bois contient un matelas et un bain intégré. Douche, toilette et lavabo se cachent derrière des portes vitrées translucides.

Este pequeño estudio de 24 m² acondicionado para una pareja muestra inteligentes y prácticas ideas de distribución. Las reducidas dimensiones reclamaban una división de los espacios por medio del uso de distintos materiales y niveles. En un lado, cerca de la entrada, la cocina recibe luz a través de unas ventanas situadas sobre la encimera. En el otro, una mesa rectangular sirve tanto de escritorio como de superficie. Sobre ésta, un estante acoge libros y diversos elementos decorativos. Una plataforma de madera contiene el colchón y un baño integrado. La ducha, inodoro y el lavamanos se esconden tras unas puertas de cristal translúcido.

Location: Paris
Architect: Guillaume Terver and Fabienne Couvert
Photos: © Vincent Leroux

All in One

This small 30 m² apartment, otherwise a regular space, is elongated by its generous ceiling height. Up until several years ago it formed part of a religious congregation of which only the door was conserved. The architect grouped together all elements in one single volume attached to the wall. A square wooden box finished in sycamore panels incorporates all the components of the residence: The bed rest justs above a closet. On one end, the door provides access to the kitchen, through which the bathroom is reached. This module also contains the television, a fold-down office table and space for electronic equipment.

Dieses kleine Apartment mit einer zwar kleinen Fläche von nur 30 m², jedoch großzügiger Höhe, gehörte bis vor einigen Jahren einer religiösen Gesellschaft, an die nur noch die Tür erinnert. Der Architekt hat alle Elemente in einem einzigen, an der Wand angelehnten, viereckigen und mit Sykomore-Paneelen verkleideten Holzkasten untergebracht. Alle Komponenten der Wohnung haben dort Platz: das Bett im oberen Teil und darunter ein Schrank. An einem Ende die Zugangstür zur Küche und von dort in das Bad. Hier stehen auch der Fernseher, ein herabklappbarer Arbeitstisch und elektronische Geräte.

All in One
Guillaume Terver and Fabienne Couvert

Ce petit appartement de 30 m² naît d'une superficie régulière, de hauteur et de largeur. Il appartenait auparavant à l'ensemble d'une congrégation dont seule la porte fut préservée. L'architecte a groupé les éléments en un seul volume adossé au mur. Il s'agit d'une caisse carrée, habillée de panneaux de sycomore. L'ensemble des pièces composant l'habitation sont abrités par cet élément : le lit, au-dessus, et l'armoire, en dessous. À un extrême, la porte d'accès de la cuisine donnant sur la salle de bain. Ce meuble accueille aussi la télévision, une table de travail abattable et des rangement pour l'électroménager.

Este pequeño apartamento de 30 m² es una superficie regular, alargada y de altura generosa. Hasta hace unos años, pertenecía a una congregación religiosa. De su antiguo uso sólo se ha conservado la puerta. El arquitecto ha agrupado todos los elementos en un solo volumen adosado a la pared. Se trata de una caja cuadrada de madera revestida con paneles de sicomoro. Todos los componentes de la vivienda están contenidos en este elemento: la cama, en la parte superior, y debajo, un armario. En un extremo, la puerta de acceso a la cocina, desde la que se accede al baño. Este mueble alberga también la televisión, una mesa abatible de trabajo y unos espacios para los equipos electrónicos.

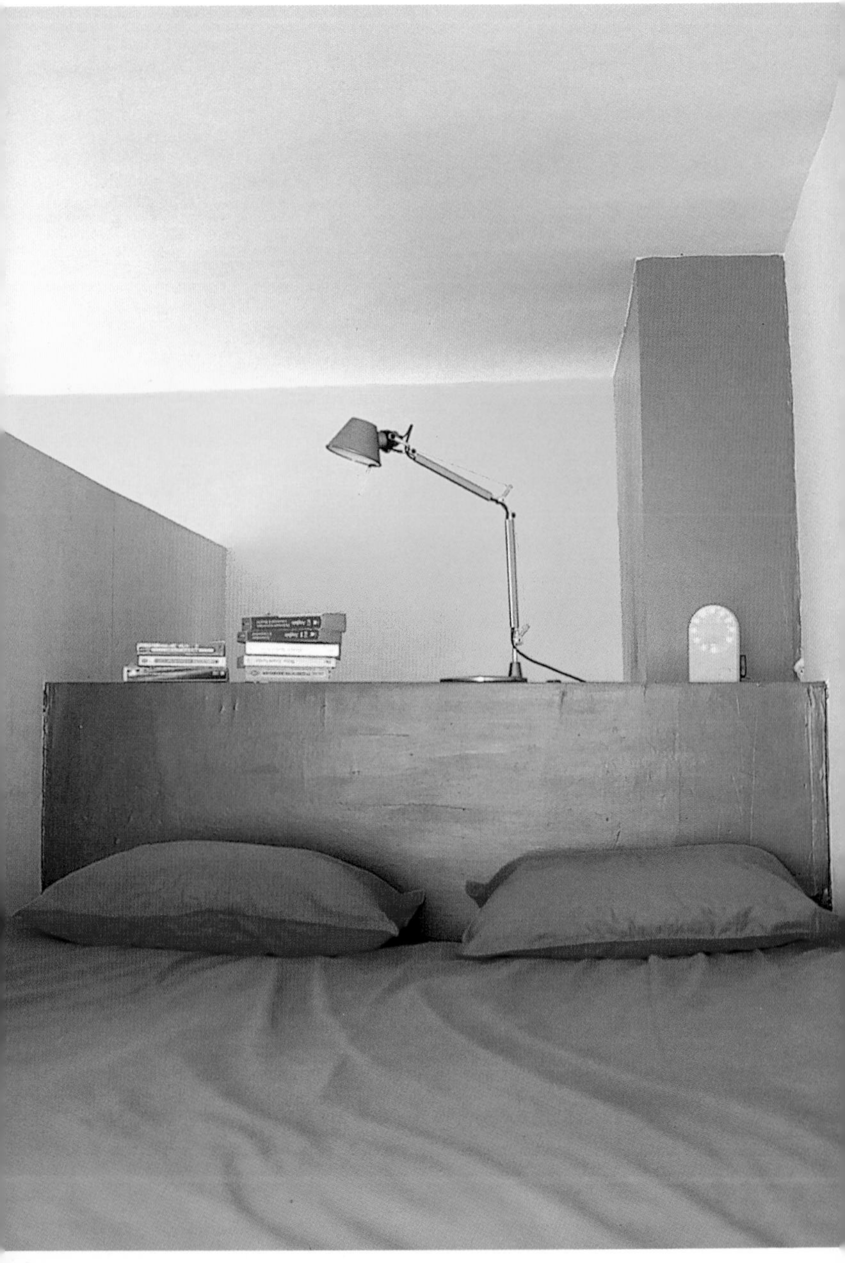

Location: 10ème Arrondissement
Interior Designer: Marie-France de Saint-Félix
Photos: © Roland Beaufre (Agence Top)
dsfcrea@aol.com

Paris White

This spacious loft uses white as the foundation for simple furniture and elegant detail. The main space is a large open area in which the living room, dining area and kitchen interact with each other. The kitchen features a bar that partly conceals the cooking area, at the same time creating a boundary between this and the lounge. A small round table acts as a snack or a breakfast table in front of the windows, and on the other corner, farther away from the sofas, a proper dining table holds enough places for 8 dinner guests. The room is kept private on the other side of the living room wall, which shares the space with an en-suite bathroom. Exposed wooden beams are treated in white to create an elegently worn appearance that adds to the feeling of comfort in this refined Parisian loft.

In diesem geräumigen Loft ist die Farbe Weiß der Ausgangspunkt für einfaches, elegant gestaltetes Mobiliar. Der Hauptbereich besteht aus einer offenen Fläche in der Wohnzimmer, Essbereich und eine Küche, die durch eine Bar in zwei Teile geteilt wird, ineinander übergehen. Ein runder Tisch vor der Fensterfront wird für das Frühstück genutzt. Gegenüber der Sofaecke steht ein Esstisch, an dem bis zu 8 Personen Platz finden. Auf der anderen Seite des Wohnzimmers befinden sich ein etwas persönlicherer Bereich und ein Bad. Weiß gestrichene Holzbalken tragen zu der eleganten und behaglichen Atmosphäre in diesem raffinierten Pariser Loft bei.

Paris White
Marie-France de Saint-Félix

Ce loft spacieux utilise le blanc comme fondation pour un mobilier simple aux détails élégants. L'espace principal est une aire ouverte où se mêlent séjour, salle à manger et cuisine et qui se divise en deux par un bar servant de table de déjeuner. À l'autre angle, éloignée de la zone sofas, une table de repas accueille jusqu'à huit commensaux. Une zone plus intime, de l'autre côté, partage l'espace avec une salle de bain complète. Des poutres de bois, traitées et teintées de blanc, parachèvent une apparence élégante, ajoutant une touche de confort à ce loft parisien raffiné.

Este espacioso loft utiliza el color blanco como fundamento para un mobiliario simple y de elegante detalle. El espacio principal es un área abierta en donde se mezclan el estar, el comedor y la cocina, que se divide en dos por medio de una barra. Una mesa redonda delante de los ventanales se utiliza para el desayuno. En una esquina, alejada de la zona de sofás, una mesa de co-medor permite albergar hasta ocho comensales. Una zona más privada al otro lado del salón comparte espacio con un baño completo. Las vigas de madera tratada y pintadas en blanco acaban por conformar una apariencia elegante que añade confort a este refinado loft parisiense.

Location: 14ème Arrondissement
Architect: Littow Architects
Photos: © Pekka Littow
littow@magic.fr

Rue Friant

In an attempt to take the most advantage of a 64 m² space, all existing partitions were eliminated except for the structural walls. In their place and to delineate the various areas, a series of islands and pillars were erected to give a sense of fluidity from one space to another. The kitchen and bathroom installations were grouped together to avoid technical difficulties. In the living room, the original brick wall was kept exposed. The bedroom is situated on the lower level and receives natural light from the ground floor windows.

Um die vorhandenen 64 m² optimal auszunutzen, wurden außer den tragenden Mauern alle übrigen entfernt. Verschiedene Bereiche werden stattdessen durch Inseln und Säulen abgegrenzt und vermitteln den Eindruck fließender Übergänge. Zur Vermeidung von technischen Schwierigkeiten wurden die Installationen von Küche und Bad zusammengelegt. Im Wohnzimmer sind die ursprünglichen Backsteinmauern unverändert erhalten. Das Schlafzimmer befindet sich im Souterrain und wird durch die auf Straßenhöhe liegenden Fenster mit Licht versorgt.

Rue Friant
Littow Architects

Pour tenter de mettre à profit le maximum d'un espace de 64 m², toutes les partitions ont été éliminées de cet appartement, hormis les murs porteurs. En leur lieu et place, pour délimiter les diverses zones, ont été conçus des îlots et piliers communiquant une sensation de fluidité entre les espaces. Afin d'éviter les difficultés techniques, les installations ont été groupées dans la cuisine et les salles de bain. Le séjour respecte les murs d'origine aux briques apparentes. La chambre à coucher se trouve au niveau inférieur et reçoit la lumière naturelle des fenêtres sur la rue.

En un intento de conseguir aprovechar al máximo un espacio de 64 m², se eliminaron todas las particiones de este apartamento, excepto los muros de carga. En su lugar y para delimitar las distintas zonas, se diseñaron unas isletas y pilares que dan sensación de fluidez entre un espacio y otro. Para evitar dificultades técnicas, se agruparon las instalaciones de la cocina y el baño. En la sala de estar se respetaron las paredes originales de ladrillo visto. El dormitorio se sitúa en el nivel inferior y recibe luz natural de las ventanas del nivel de la calle.

Location: 3ème Arrondissement
Architect: Babel Architecture
Photos: © Deidi Von Schaewen
babelarchitecture@wanadoo.fr

Sculptural Elements

An apartment bursting with personality, reminiscent of a theater set, has been created to cater to both the demands imposed by the dimensions and specific characteristics of the building and the needs of the owners. False walls and imposing forms –such as the large circular element that dominates the entire setting– serve to define the various spaces that make up the apartment while also providing the visual axis around which the space is organized. The exuberant character of this architectural project is complemented by decorative features that skillfully draw on a wide variety of styles. This visual richness, allied with the use of noble materials, contrasts beautifully with the austerity of the color scheme.

Hier wurde eine Wohnung mit Persönlichkeit geschaffen, die sich einerseits an die Dimensionen und Eigenarten des Gebäudes anpasst und andererseits den Ansprüchen der Eigentümer entspricht. Unwirkliche Wände und schwergewichtige Elemente – wie diese Rundmauer –, die die verschiedenen Wohnbereiche des Apartments miteinander verbinden und gleichzeitig die visuellen Achsen der Raumaufteilung sind. Eine gelungene Lösung des Architekten, der für die Dekoration stilistischen Reichtum und die Verwendung edler Materialien in Gegensatz zu chromatischer Strenge gesetzt hat.

Sculptural Elements
Babel Architecture

Michel Seban et Élisabeth Douillet ont été chargés de réhabiliter cet espace. Comme au théâtre, ils ont créé une demeure à la vive personnalité s'adaptant aux exigences, dimensions et particularismes de l'immeuble, et aux impératifs des propriétaires. Parois irréelles et volumes pesants – tel l'élément circulaire envahissant le lieu – se chargent de régler les différentes pièces composant le logement tout en devenant l'axe visuel organisant l'espace. Un exercice d'architecture de caractère dont la décoration repose sur un judicieux mélange de tendances. Richesse stylistique et matériaux nobles contrastent agréablement avec l'austérité chromatique.

Como si de la escenografía de una representación teatral se tratara se ha creado una vivienda llena de personalidad que se adapta tanto a las exigencias que las dimensiones y particularidades del inmueble le imponen como a las necesidades de los propietarios. Paredes irreales y volúmenes rotundos –como el gran elemento circular que invade el ambiente– se encargan de resolver las diferentes estancias que conforman la casa, a la vez que se convierten en el eje visual a través del cual se organiza el espacio. Un ejercicio de arquitectura lleno de carácter cuya decoración se ha resuelto empleando una acertada mezcla de tendencias. La riqueza estilística y el empleo de materiales nobles contrastan gratamente con la austeridad cromática.

Location: 4ème Arrondissement
Architect: Barclay and Crousse
Photos: © J.P. Crousse
archi22@club-internet.fr

Essential and White

The apartment is located in a 17th century building found in the heart of the Marais of Paris. Its reduced 32 m² surface area and thick structural wall dividing it in two orientated the architect's difficult task. All the elements added to the original structure were conceived as furniture pieces to avoid reducing the spatial dimensions laid down by the existing structure. The open-plan kitchen facing the living room was designed as an element with pure forms that folds vertically, transforming itself into a shelf and folding once again against the ceiling to indicate the entrance and the fireplace.

Das Apartment befindet sich in einem Gebäude aus dem 17. Jahrhundert, im Herzen des Marais. Bei der Gestaltung richteten sich die Architekten nach den geringen Abmessungen (32 m²) und den durch eine massive tragende Mauer, die die Wohnung in zwei Bereiche teilt, entstehenden Schwierigkeiten. Alle der ursprünglichen Struktur hinzugefügten Elemente wurden als Möbel entworfen, um zu vermeiden, dass die Ausmaße des vorhandenen Raumes verringert werden. Die Küche öffnet sich zum Wohnzimmer. Neben ihr erhebt sich ein schlichtes Element bis zur Decke, das in ein Regal übergeht sowie den Eingang und den Kamin definiert.

Essential and White
Barclay and Crousse

L'appartement habite un immeuble XVIIème, au cœur du Marais. Une superficie réduite (32 m²) et l'écueil d'un épais mur porteur divisant le lieu en deux ont orienté les architectes vers un travail sur l'espace. Tous les éléments ajoutés à la structure d'origine ont été conçus comme des meubles, pour éviter de réduire les dimensions imposées par la structure préexistante. La cuisine ouverte sur le salon a été pensée comme un élément formellement pur, pliable d'abord verticalement pour devenir étagère puis à nouveau contre le plafond pour signaler l'entrée et l'espace cheminée.

El apartamento está situado en un edificio del siglo XVII, en pleno corazón del Marais. Su reducida superficie (32 m²) y la dificultad que supone un grueso muro portante que lo divide en dos orientó el trabajo de los arquitectos sobre el espacio. Todos los elementos añadidos a la estructura de origen han sido concebidos como muebles, evitando reducir las dimensiones espaciales dadas por la estructura existente. La cocina abierta hacia el salón ha sido diseñada como un elemento de formas puras que se recoge verticalmente, transformándose en estantería, y plegándose nuevamente contra el cielo raso para señalar la entrada y el espacio de la chimenea.

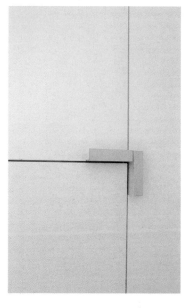

Location: 3ème Arrondissement
Architect: Gil Percal
Photos: © Gilles Gustève

Unifying Factor

This space constituted two independent floors, the fifth and sixth floor of a building in the 3rd arrondissement of Paris. The architect created an access communicating both levels, gaining enough space for an extra bedroom. The intervention resulted in a 130 m² surface area and an important articulating axis: the union of the two levels by way of a monumental staircase that occupies the whole entrance area of the apartment. This element is also the support for the upper floor's framework and conceals a metallic pillar on the left side.

Der Architekt entwarf einen Zugang, der die fünfte und die sechste Etage in einem Gebäude des 3. Bezirks von Paris miteinander verbindet und so Raum für ein weiteres Zimmer schafft. Dadurch entstand eine Wohnfläche von 130 m² um eine zentrale Achse herum: die Verbindung zweier Ebenen über eine monumentale Treppe, die den gesamten Eingang zum Apartment ausfüllt, die Decke der oberen Etage trägt und gleichzeitig eine Metallsäule auf der linken Seite verbirgt.

Unifying Factor
Gil Percal

Cet espace appartenait à deux étages indépendants, le cinquième et le sixième d'un immeuble du 3° arrondissement. L'architecte a créé un accès faisant communiquer les deux niveaux, gagnant un espace pour une nouvelle pièce. De cette intervention naît une superficie de 130 m² et un axe d'articulation essentiel : l'union des deux niveaux par un escalier monumental occupant toute l'entrée de l'appartement. Cet élément est, en outre, le support de l'étage supérieur et dissimule une colonne métallique sur son flanc droit.

Este espacio está constituido por dos plantas antaño independientes, la quinta y la sexta, de un edificio del distrito 3 de París. El arquitecto creó un acceso que comunicaba ambas plantas, con lo que se gana espacio para una habitación más. De la intervención resulta una superficie de 130 m² y un eje articulador importante: la unión de los dos niveles mediante una escalera monumental que ocupa toda la entrada del apartamento. Este elemento, además, es el soporte del forjado de la planta superior y disimula una columna metálica en el lado izquierdo.

Location: 19ème Arrondissement
Architect: Alain Salomon
Photos: © Chris Tubbs, Alain Salomon
apsalomon@wanadoo.fr

Loft Complex

Close to the Porte de Pantin, this 150 m² loft belongs to an actor and his wife. The space forms part of a complex of 30 lofts created for a community of artists. The interiors are distributed on three floors: the street level (with a garage), the entrance (accessible by way of a patio), and the attic. An internal staircase links the office and the garage with the living space, where an impressive living/dining room space opens out to a kitchen, an extra bathroom and a guest bedroom which is used as a daily breakfast room.

Nahe der Porte de Pantin liegt dieser 150 m² Loft eines Schauspielers und seiner Frau. Er gehört zu einem aus 30 Lofts bestehenden Gebäudekomplex, der für eine Künstlergemeinschaft gebaut wurde. Die Innenräume sind jeweils in drei Ebenen unterteilt: eine auf Straßenhöhe (mit Garage), der Eingangsbereich (in den man durch den Innenhof des Gebäudes gelangt) und ein Zwischengeschoss. Eine Treppe im Inneren verbindet Büro und Garage mit der Wohnung, deren Besonderheit ein doppelt raumhohes Wohnzimmer mit Essecke ist und die fernerhin aus einer offenen Küche, einem Gästebad und einem Gästezimmer besteht, in dem zugleich jeden Tag gefrühstückt wird.

Loft Complex
Alain Salomon

Près de la porte de Pantin, le loft de 150 m² d'un acteur de cinéma et de son épouse forme partie d'un ensemble de 30 lofts créés pour une communauté d'artistes. Les intérieurs sont distribués sur trois niveaux : la rue (avec un garage), l'entrée (accessible depuis le patio de l'immeuble) et des combles. Un escalier intérieur relie le bureau et le garage avec les pièces du niveau supérieur. Prennent ici la vedette une double espace séjour/salle à manger, une cuisine ouverte, une salle de bain de complément et une chambre d'hôte, qui joue au quotidien la salle de déjeuner.

Cercano a la puerta de Pantín, este loft de 150 m² pertenece a un actor de cine y a su mujer. El espacio forma parte de un grupo de 30 lofts creados para una comunidad de artistas. Los interiores se dividen en tres niveles: el de la calle (con un garaje), el de la entrada (al que se accede desde el patio del edificio) y un altillo. Una escalera interior conecta la oficina y el garaje con la vivienda, donde destaca un doble espacio de sala de estar y el comedor, una cocina abierta, un baño complementario y una habitación de invitados, que se utiliza como lugar para el desayuno en el día a día.

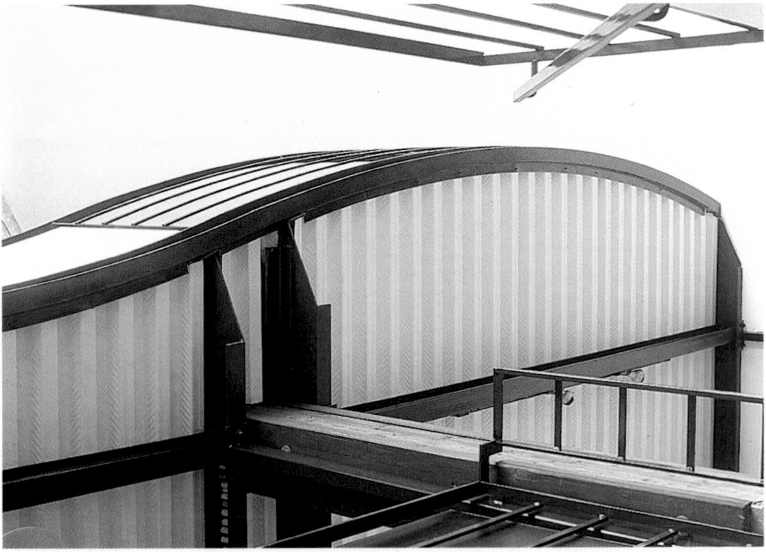

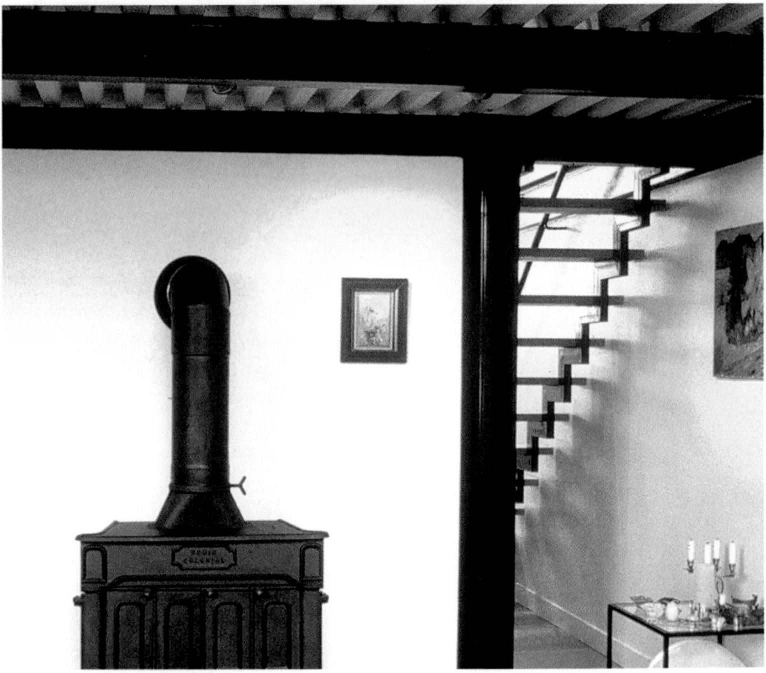

Location: 4ème Arrondissement
Architect: Danielle Hollando and Yves Sebagh
Photos: © Olivier Hallot
jefka.archi@free.fr
sbco@clubinternet.fr

In the Marais

The original palace in which this apartment is located is a beautiful example of Parisian 18th century architecture. From the outside, an impressive staircase adorned by a fresco, and a great iron clad handrail pay testimony to the building's antiquity. Upon entering the apartment, another universe emerges, both architectural and contemporary. It is composed of two levels: a living room occupies the ground floor while the kitchen, bedroom and bathroom are situated in the basement. In the living room, architects have played with cornices and false plaster ceilings to structure the space. In the bedroom a plaster headrest also serves as a shelf space. The rigour of this 1940's inspired architecture is softened with the presence of curved glass-brick walls.

Die Wohnung befindet sich in einer Villa, einem schönen Beispiel der Pariser Architektur des 18. Jahrhunderts. Am Eingang sind der imponierende, freskendekorierte Treppenschacht und das schmiedeeiserne Geländer Zeugen vergangener Pracht. Beim Eintritt in die Wohnung öffnet sich eine architektonisch andere moderne Welt auf zwei Ebenen: im Erdgeschoss ein großes Wohnzimmer, im Untergeschoss Küche, Schlafzimmer und Bad. Im Wohnzimmer strukturierten die Architekten den Raum mit Obersimsen und Zwischendecken. Die Strenge dieser aus den 40er Jahren inspirierten Architektur wird durch geschwungene Wände aus Glasbausteinen gemildert.

In the Marais
Danielle Hollando and Yves Sebagh

L'hôtel particulier dans lequel se suite cet appartement, est un bel exemple de l'architecture parisienne du XVIIIe siècle. Lorsqu'on arrive de l'extérieur, l'imposante cage d'escalier décorée de fresque et une superb rampe en fer forgé témoignent de l'ancienneté du lieu. En entrant dans l'appartement, on bascule dans un tout autre univers, architectureé et contemporain. Il este composé de deux niveaux: un vaste séjour ocupe le rez-de-jardin, la cuisine, la chambre et la salle de bain étant situées sous-plafonds en staff qui structurent l'espace. La rigueur de cette architecture d'inspiration 40, est tempérée par la présence de cloisons courbes en briques de verre. Dans la chambre une tête de lit en staff sert à la fois de chevets et d'étagères.

El palacete en el que se encuentra el apartamento es un bello ejemplo de la arquitectura parisiense del siglo XVIII. La imponente caja de la escalera decorada con un fresco y una gran barandilla en hierro forjado testimonia la antigüedad del edificio. Al acceder al apartamento, se entra en otro universo, arquitectónico y contemporáneo. Está compuesto por dos niveles: un gran estar ocupa la planta baja, mientras que la cocina, la habitación y el baño se sitúan en el subsuelo. En el salón, los arquitectos han pensado todo un juego de cornisas y falsos techos que estructuran el espacio. El rigor de esta arquitectura de inspiración años 40 se templa con la presencia de paredes curvas de ladrillos de vidrio. En el dormitorio una cabecera de obra sirve también como estantería.

Location: 5ème Arrondissement
Architect: Andrée Putman
Photos: © Roland Beaufre (Agence Top)
Fax: +33 1 55 42 88 50

White Foundation

This apartment-loft demonstrates enormous skill in putting its dimensions and characteristics to good use. Painted in white to emphasize luminosity and visually enlarge the space, the residence utilizes a series of solutions and stylistic resources that serve as a backdrop for the furniture and fresh objects found in the calm and neutral interior. The result is a relaxing, sober and inspiring atmosphere. An open space features large windows that communicate the interior with the exterior garden that envelops the house and which at the same time captivates one's attention, while natural light invades and bounces of the whiteness that shrouds every corner.

In diesem loftartigen Apartment wurden die vorhandenen Ausmaße und Eigenschaften sehr geschickt genutzt. Um die Helligkeit zu betonen und den Raum optisch zu vergrößern, wurden die Wände weiß gestrichen. Zahlreiche Lösungsansätze und Stilmittel bilden den Hintergrund für das Mobiliar und die frischen und zeitlosen Design-Objekte aus denen diese im wesentlichen ruhige und neutrale Einrichtung besteht. Das Ergebnis ist eine entspannende, zurückhaltende und anregende Atmosphäre. Große Fenster verbinden den offenen Innenraum mit dem das Haus umgebenden Garten und ziehen die Aufmerksamkeit auf sich, während das Tageslicht einfällt und von dem in allen Winkeln vorhandenen Weiß zurückgeworfen wird.

White Foundation
Andrée Putman

Ce loft souligne une certaine expertise quant aux dimensions et aux caractéristiques de l'espace. Vêtu de blanc pour optimiser la luminosité et l'amplitude visuelle, le logement joue sur un répertoire de solutions et de ressources offrant une toile de fond au mobilier et aux objets design, frais et atemporels, sur lesquels repose cet intérieur essentiellement neutre et serein. Est née une ambiance relaxante, sobre et inspirée. Un espace ouvert où les vastes baies associent l'intérieur avec le jardin extérieur qui l'entoure et saisissent parallèlement l'attention. La lumière naturelle s'infiltre et ricoche sur le blanc couvrant les moindres recoins.

Este apartamento-loft demuestra una enorme pericia a la hora de aprovechar las dimensiones y las características que el espacio brindaba. Pintada de blanco para enfatizar la luminosidad y potenciar la amplitud visual, la vivienda utiliza un repertorio de soluciones y recursos estilísticos que sirven de telón de fondo al mobiliario y los objetos de diseño fresco y atemporal en los que se basa este interior esencialmente neutro y sosegado. El resultado es una atmósfera relajante, sobria e inspiradora. Un espacio abierto en el que grandes ventanales comunican el interior con el jardín exterior que rodea la casa y que se encargan, al mismo tiempo, de captar irresistiblemente la atención mientras la luz natural invade y rebota con el blanco que cubre todos los rincones.

Location: St. Cloud
Architect: Annie Verlant
Photos: © Olivier Hallot
gverlant@bygcollector.com

Heights of St. Cloud

The privilege granted by this 130 m² apartment is its formidable view over Paris. Any of the rooms in the space –the living room, bedroom, or even the bathroom– provide views of the Bois de Boulogne, the Seine river and most clearly of the Eiffel Tower. Hypnotic sunsets can be admired from the bathtub; early evenings are magical. Situated in a neoclassical building from the 1930´s, the space was transformed to acquire a comfortably-proportioned living/dining room. The large entrance was converted into a bedroom that doubles as an office, as a living room when the furniture is rearranged and as meeting point for luggage on the way out for a trip.

Das große Privileg dieses 130 m² großen Apartments ist sein phantastischer Blick über Paris. Alle Zimmer geben den Blick frei auf den Bois de Boulogne, die Seine und sogar den Eiffelturm. Von der Badewanne aus kann man absolut magische Dämmerung und Sonnenuntergänge bewundern! Das Apartment in einem neoklassischen Gebäude aus den 30er Jahren wurde in ein Wohn-Esszimmer mit angenehmen Proportionen verwandelt. Der große Eingang wurde zu einem Zimmer, das gleichzeitig als Büro, bei Umgruppierung der Stühle auch als kleines Wohnzimmer, benutzt werden kann, sowie als Treffpunkt der Koffer bei der Abreise.

Heights of St. Cloud
Annie Verlant

Le grand privilège de cet appartement de 130 m² est la formidable vue qu´il a sur Paris. Quelque soit la pièce où l´on se trouve, le salon, la chambre ou encore la salle de bain, on peut profiter de la vue sur le Bois de Boulogne, la Seine, et surtout sur la Tour Eiffel. On peut assister à d´hypnotiques couchers de soleil à partir de la baignoire. Le soir c´est absolument magique. Situé dans un immeuble néo-classique des années trente, ce lieu a subi quelques transformations pour offrir un salon-salle à manger avec des proportions confortables. L´entrée disproportionée est devenue une véritable pièce à vivre. Elle fait office de bureau, de petit salon quand les chaises viennent s´ajouter au guéridon, et de point de rencontre avec les bagages les jours de départ en voyage.

El gran privilegio de este apartamento de 130 m² es la formidable vista sobre París. Sea cual sea la habitación en la que nos encontremos, el salón, el dormitorio o incluso el baño, se puede disfrutar de la vista sobre el Bois de Boulogne, el Sena y sobre todo la Torre Eiffel. Se puede asistir a hipnóticas puestas de sol desde la bañera. Los atardeceres son absolutamente mágicos. Situado en un edificio neoclásico de los años treinta, este lugar ha sido transformado para conseguir un salón comedor de proporciones confortables. La entrada, escesivamente grande, se ha convertido en una verdadera habitación para vivir. Hace las veces de escritorio, de pequeño salón cuando las sillas se agrupan y de punto de encuentro con las maletas al partir de viaje.

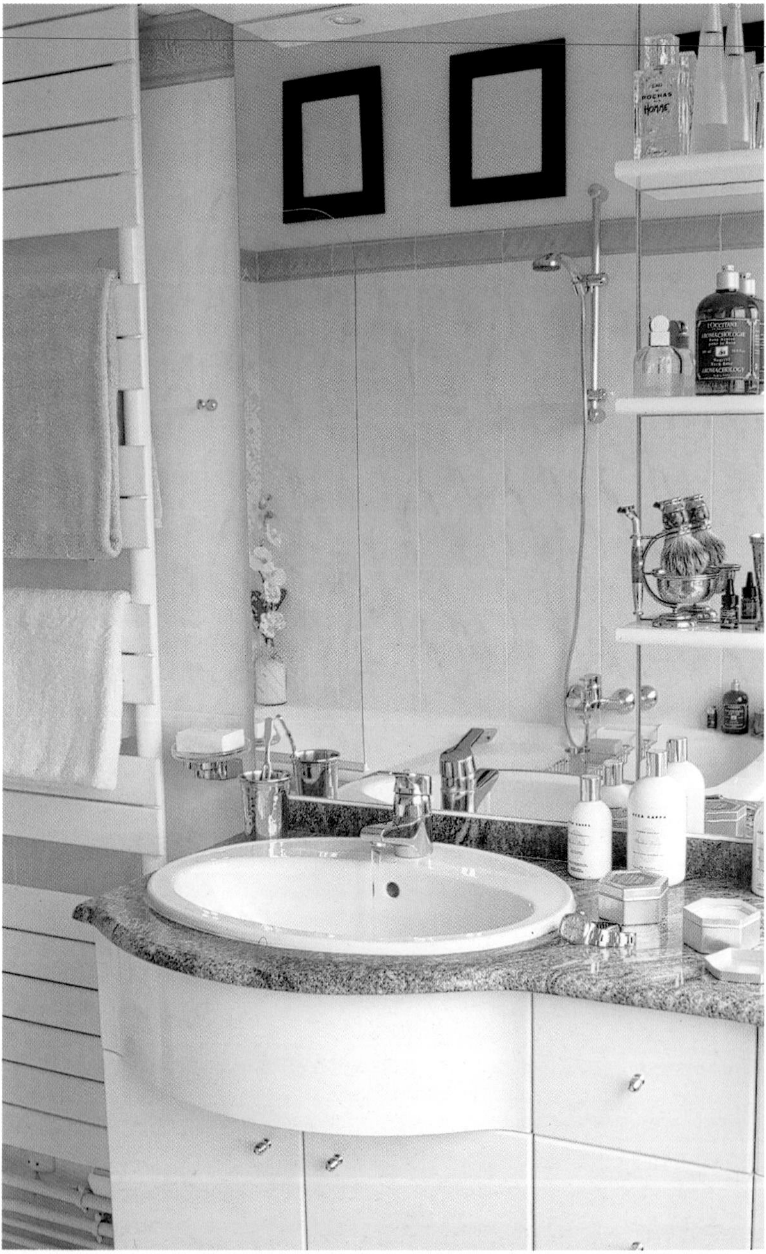
ROCHAS
HOMME
L'OCCITANE
AROMACHOLOGIE

Location: 9ème Arrondissement
Architect: Caroline Chapus
Photos: © Olivier Hallot
Tel: +33 1 69 95 38 75

In Montmartre

What at one time was an apartment with three service rooms, ceramicist Caroline Chapus transformed into a space for relaxed living. The 100 m² distributed over two levels contain the family home and a studio. The family interacts on the lower level, in the living room, kitchen and the Mediterranean-style dining room, where light is constant and the walls are oil-painted in sunflower yellow. In the kitchen, a whole wall is covered by a chalkboard, so that the children can have free reign of expression. The wicker baskets and stars created by Caroline add a touch of humor. The upper level houses three bedrooms, a bathroom and the studio. The studio has its own door, offering privacy to its occupant.

Die Keramikerin Caroline Chapus schuf einen entspannenden Raum aus einem früheren Apartment mit drei Zimmern. Die auf zwei Ebenen verteilten 100 m² beherbergen Raum für die Familie und eine Werkstatt. Alle Welt trifft sich im Wohnzimmer und der Wohnküche der unteren Ebene mit mediterranen Akzenten, wo den ganzen Tag hindurch Licht einfällt. Ein Teil der Küchenwand ist mit Schiefer verkleidet zur freien Benutzung für die Kinder. Von Caroline hergestellte Sterne und Sonnen aus Weidengeflecht vermitteln gute Laune. Auf der zweiten Ebene befinden sich drei Zimmer, ein kleines Bad und die Werkstatt mit eigener Eingangstür.

In Montmartre
Caroline Chapus

Dans un appartement et trois chambres de service, la céramiste Caroline Chapus a créé un lieu de vie décontracté. Les 100 m² disposés sur deux niveaux abritent la famille et un atelier. Tout le monde se réunit au niveau inférieur dans le salon et dans la cuisine-salle à manger aux accents méditerranéens. Cette dernière est lumineuse à tous les instants de la journée avec ses murs bouton d'or tamponnés avec de la peinture à l'huile. Une partie du mur de la cuisine est recouvert de peinture à tableau noir. Des étoiles et soleils en osier réalisés par Caroline apportent leur touche d'humour. Le second niveau accueille trois chambres, une petite salle de bain et l'atelier. Il garantit à ses occupants une certaine autonomie puisqu'il est doté de sa propre porte d'entrée.

En lo que en otra época era un apartamento y tres habitaciones de servicio, la ceramista Caroline Chapus creó un espacio de vida relajado. Los 100 m² dispuestos en dos niveles albergan los espacios domésticos y un taller. Todo el mundo se reúne en el nivel inferior, en el salón y en la cocina-comedor con acentos mediterráneos. Esta última es luminosa durante todo el día con sus paredes estampadas con óleo. Una parte de la pared de la cocina está recubierta con pizarra. Aquí los niños pueden expresarse libremente. Estrellas y soles de mimbre realizados por Caroline aportan un toque de humor. El segundo nivel acoge tres habitaciones, un pequeño baño y el taller. Éste garantiza a sus ocupantes una cierta autonomía ya que posee su propia puerta de entrada.

caillou
genou
chou

hibou
joujou
pou

$1 = 9$
$2 = 18$
$3 = 27$
$4 = 15$

Location: Montmorency
Architect: Frédérique Chandy
Photos: © Olivier Hallot

In Montmorency

This house in Montmorency appears to protect itself from modern urban life. The house feels like a vacation house, both cheerful and cozy, thanks to the benevolent talent of Frédérique Chandy. This artist, who creates all kind of decorative objects, exhibits a home full of color with a certain air of Mediterranean lifestlye. Light floods in through the french windows that open out onto a stone terrace and garden. The yellow and blue of the sun, sea and sky are represented on the walls, fabrics and objects that adorn the house, as if inviting one on a journey. Painting becomes another important influence for the decoration. The paintings, just as much as the painted furniture, integrate with the subtle style of an artist with a passion for harmony.

Dieses Haus in Montmorency scheint sich vor dem modernen Stadtleben zu schützen. Dank dem optimistischen Talent Frédérique Chandys wurde das Heim zu einem fröhlichen und gemütlichen Ferienhaus. Diese Künstlerin dekorativer Gegenstände präsentiert ein Haus voller Farben mit einem gewissen Flair mediterranen Lebensstils. Durch die Glastüren zur steinernen Terrasse und zum Garten flutet reichlich Licht herein. Überall an den Wänden, den Stoffen und Gegenständen leuchtet das Gelb der Sonne, das Blau des Meeres und des Himmels. Dazu kommen die Gemälde und die lackierten Möbel als integrierender Teil dieser Leidenschaft für Harmonie.

In Montmorency
Frédérique Chandy

Cette maison de Montmorency semble se préserver de la vie citadine moderne. Elle a su se faire gaie, accueillante, comme une maison de vacances, grâce au talent bienveillant de Frédérique Chandy. Cette artiste, qui réalise toutes sortes d'objets pour l'art de la table, exprime chez elle un style qui autorise tous les effets de couleurs subtilement mariées à un certain art de vivre trés méditerranéen. Les portes-fenêtres s'ouvrent de plain-pied sur une terrasse dallée de pierres, prolongée par une pelouse. Le jaune du soleil, le bleu de la mer et du ciel sont omniprésents sur les murs, les tissus, les objets, comme une invitation au voyage. Autre influence, également celle de la peinture. Tableaux, mais aussi meubles peints, s'intègrent au décor de cette passionnée d'harmonies.

Esta vivienda de Montmorency parece resguardarse de la vida moderna de la ciudad. Se ha sabido alegrarla, hacerla acogedora, como una casa de vacaciones, gracias al talento benévolo de Frédérique Chandy. Esta artista, que crea todo tipo de objetos para el arte de la mesa, muestra en su casa un estilo que da cabida a todos los efectos de color sutilmente aliados a un cierto arte de vida muy mediterráneo. La luz entra a raudales, por las cristaleras que se abren a una terraza enlosada con piedra, que se prolonga en cesped. El amarillo del sol, el azul del mar y del cielo están omnipresentes en las paredes, las telas, los objetos, como una invitación al viaje. La pintura es también otra influencia. Los cuadros, así como los muebles pintados, integran el decorado sutil de esta artista apasionada de las armonías.

Location: 16ème Arrondissement
Architect: Guillaume Henrion
Photos: © Olivier Hallot

Porte d'Auteuil

Situated in an elegant 1930's build-ing, this artist's studio is accessed by an entrance on the ground floor. The astonishing height of the six meter ceil-ing dilates the sensation of space. Its surface area reaches 200 m^2 after hav-ing added a large studio. Architect Guillaume Henrion arranged the space into a bedroom, wardrobe and large bathroom. A new staircase completes this spacious volume. Despite its gener-ous size, the homeowner still believes that the kitchen's dimensions are too modest to consider it functional.

Zu dem in einem eleganten Gebäu-de von 1930 gelegenen Künstler-studio führt der Eingang durch das Erd-geschoss. Überraschend wirken die etwa 6 Meter hohen Decken, die der Raumempfindung absolute Weite ver-leihen. Nach Anschluss eines großen Studios beträgt die Fläche 200 m^2. Der Architekt Guillaume Henrion richtete hier ein Schlafzimmer, einen Ankleide-raum und ein großes Bad ein. Eine neue Treppe vervollständigt den weit-läufigen Raum. Die Hausherrin meint jedoch, dass die Küche zu klein ist, um wirklich funktionell genutzt zu werden.

Porte d'Auteuil
Guillaume Henrion

On pénètre dans cet atelier d'artis-te, situé dans une élégante construction des années mille neuf cent trente, par une entrée en rez de jardin. Démblée, on est frappé par la hauteur sous plafond d'environ six mètres qui dilate totalement la sensation d'espa-ce. Sa superficie est de 200 mètres car-rés depuis qu'un grand studio a été acheté puis annexé. Il a été aménagé en chambre à coucher, dressing et grand salle de bain par l'architecte Guillaume Henrion. Un nouvel escalier est venu compléter ce spacieux volu-me. Toutefois, selon la maîtresse de maison, la cuisine offre des dimensions trop modestes pour être pleinement fonctionelle.

A este taller de artista, situado en una elegante construcción de 1930, se accede por una entrada situada en la planta baja. Sorprende la altura de los techos, de unos seis metros, que agran-da totalmente la sensación de espacio. Su superficie se amplió a 200 m^2 tras añadirle un gran estudio anexo. El ar-quitecto Guillaume Henrion lo arregló como dormitorio, vestidor, y un gran baño. Una nueva escalera completa el espacioso volumen. De todas formas, según el propietario, la cocina tiene di-mensiones demasiado modestas para ser completamente funcional.

Location: West Paris
Architect: Arcady
Photos: © Mihail Moldoveanu

Artist Arcady took the possibility of investing in the upper floor of his family home to better the living space of his children by "inventing" an architecture that seemed to have always been there. While he and his wife remained in the same space they had before, their adolescent children benefitted from a space adapted to their needs and to the geometry of the structure. The two levels are linked by a staircase which begins in the "antique" living room, whose style is perfectly integrated into the architecture of the 20th century building. Daylight floods the space and simple, comfortable furniture contributes to the warm atmosphere that exists. And apart from this, it is a space adapted to the landscape that surrounds it: the picturesque roofs of West Paris.

Der Künstler Arcady verschönerte in der oberen Etage seiner Wohnung den Lebensraum seiner Kinder und "erfand" dazu eine Architektur, die schon immer da gewesen zu sein scheint. Während er und seine Frau auf gleichem Raum weiterleben, genießen die Kinder die ihnen angepassten Räumlichkeiten. Beide Ebenen werden über eine Treppe verbunden, die im "alten" Wohnzimmer beginnt und in die Architektur des Gebäudes aus dem 20. Jahrhundert integriert ist. Es fällt reichlich Tageslicht in die Räume, das Mobiliar ist einfach und bequem und schafft eine warme Atmosphäre. Eine Wohnung in Harmonie mit den malerischen Dächern von West-Paris.

West Paris
Arcady

Pour accueillir sa famille, l'artiste Arcady a fait bon usage de l'aménagement de ses combles, afin d'améliorer le cadre de vie des enfants. Il a "inventé" une architecture semblant avoir toujours été présente. Le couple restant dans l'espace pré-existant, les adolescents ont hérité d'un lieu répondant à leurs besoins. Les deux niveaux sont liés par un escalier, dont une première rampe figure bien dans "l'ancien" séjour, qui s'inscrit parfaitement dans l'architecture XXème identifiant l'immeuble. L'espace généreusement baigné de lumière naturelle et le mobilier simple et confortable participent de l'ambiance chaleureuse du lieu. Par surcroît, l'appartement se fond dans son paysage : les merveilleux toits de l'ouest parisien.

Este apartamento es la vivienda familiar del artista Arcady, que ha sabido aprovechar al máximo la reforma de la buhardilla, con el fin de mejorar el habitat de sus hijos. Arcady inventó una arquitectura que parece haber estado siempre allí. Mientras que él y su mujer ocupan el espacio preexistente, los niños disfrutan de un espacio adaptado a sus necesidades. Los dos niveles están conectados por una escalera cuyo primer tramo se encuentra en el "antiguo" salón, acomodándose a la arquitectura del edificio del siglo XX. La luz del día entra abundantemente en el espacio; el mobiliario simple y confortable contribuye a la atmósfera cálida del lugar. Además es un apartamento adaptado al paisaje que lo rodea: los bellísimos tejados del oeste parisiense.

Location: Paris
Architect: Alexandre Negoescu
Photos: © Mihail Moldoveanu

Screen Room

Inspired by the 1930´s character of the apartment building and the owner´s taste and love for cinema, architect Alexandre Negoescu created a very refined space faithful to the location as well as to the logic of common sense. A vast living room is visible from the entrance door, where the furniture suggests the various functions of the space: the vestibule, foyer, dining room, an ample living room where movies can be projected, and an office area. Most of the furniture was conceived specifically for this project. The sofas and armchairs are reminiscent of the 50´s, while the dining table is a tribute to the celebrated French designers of the 1930´s. The tones and materials unify the composition of the space. In contrast to this more formal harmony, the children´s quarter is very colorful.

Inspiriert vom Gebäude aus den 30er Jahren und der Vorliebe des Eigentümers für Filme, gestaltete der Architekt eine raffinierte Atmosphäre. Vom Eingang geht der Blick in das Wohnzimmer längs der Fassade. Niedrige Möbel deuten die verschiedenen Funktionen dieses Raumes an: Vorhalle, Esszimmer, ein weitläufiger Wohnraum mit der Möglichkeit, Filme vorzuführen, und etwas abseits ein Arbeitstisch. Dazu die Möbel: Sofas und Sessel im Stil der 50er Jahre, der Esszimmertisch kokettiert mit den berühmten französischen Designern der 30er Jahre. Und im Gegensatz zu dieser nüchternen Harmonie, das Reich der Kinder in kräftigen Farben.

Screen Room
Alexandre Negoescu

Inspiré par l'immeuble années 30 et la cinéphilie du propriétaire, l'architecte Alexandre Negoescu a créé une ambiance raffinée, respectueuse du lieu et du bon sens. Visible depuis l'entrée, un vaste salon accueille des meubles bas suggérant les diverses fonctions de l'espace : vestibule, accueil, salle à manger, grand séjour/salle de projection et, en retrait, un bureau. L'essentiel du mobilier a été conçu précisément pour ce projet : des sofas et fauteuils années 50 à la table de la salle à manger, clin d'œil aux créateurs français des années 30. Moulures et matériaux offrent une harmonie formelle à cet espace, contrastant avec le coin des enfants, plus coloré.

Inspirado por el carácter de los años 30 del edificio y por el gusto cinéfilo del propietario, el arquitecto supo crear una atmósfera muy refinada respetando el espíritu del lugar. Desde la puerta de entrada se puede ver un salón que ocupa toda la longitud de la fachada. Unos muebles bajos sugieren las diversas funciones de este espacio: el vestíbulo, el comedor, el amplio salón que permite también hacer proyecciones de cine y, en un apartado, una zona de trabajo. Los muebles han sido concebidos para este proyecto: los sofás y los sillones recuerdan los años 50, mientras que la mesa del comedor es un guiño a los célebres diseñadores franceses de los años 30. En contraste con esta armonía sobria, el rincón de los niños está muy colorido.

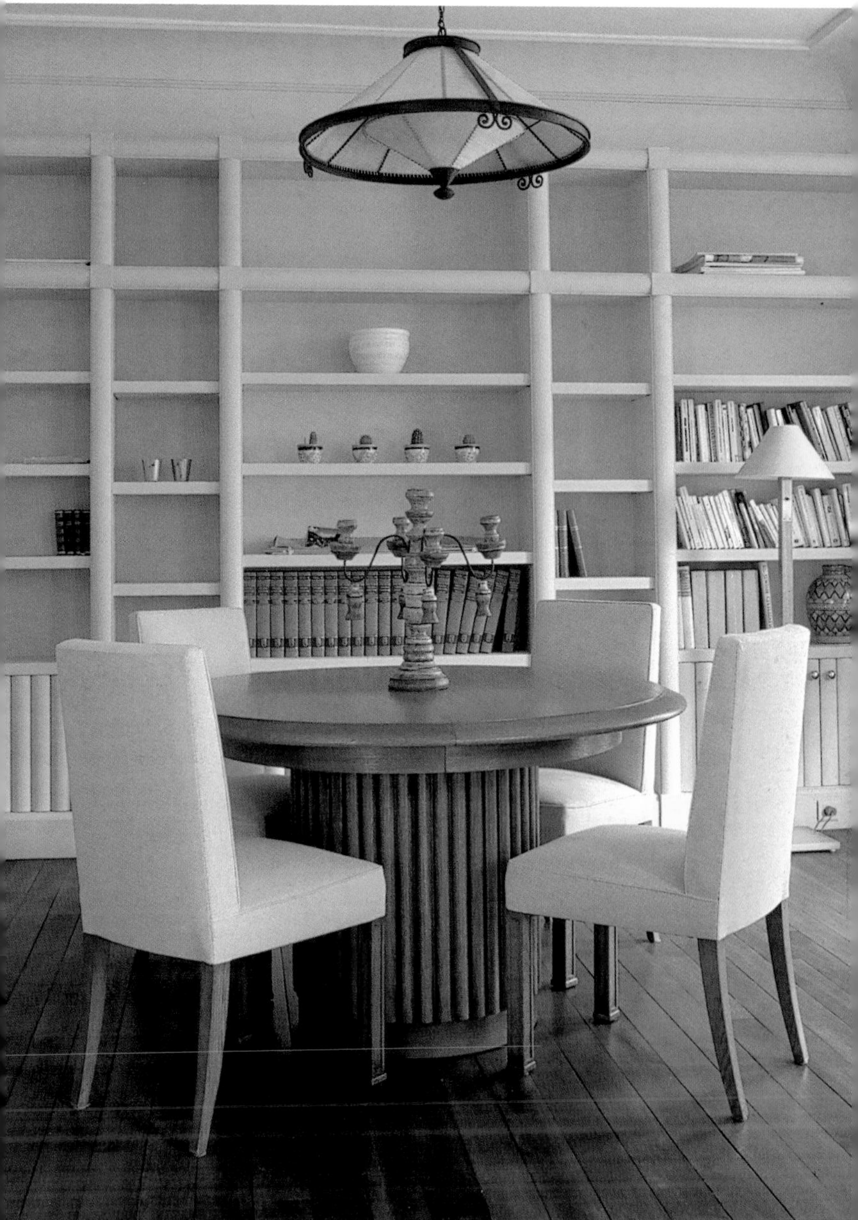

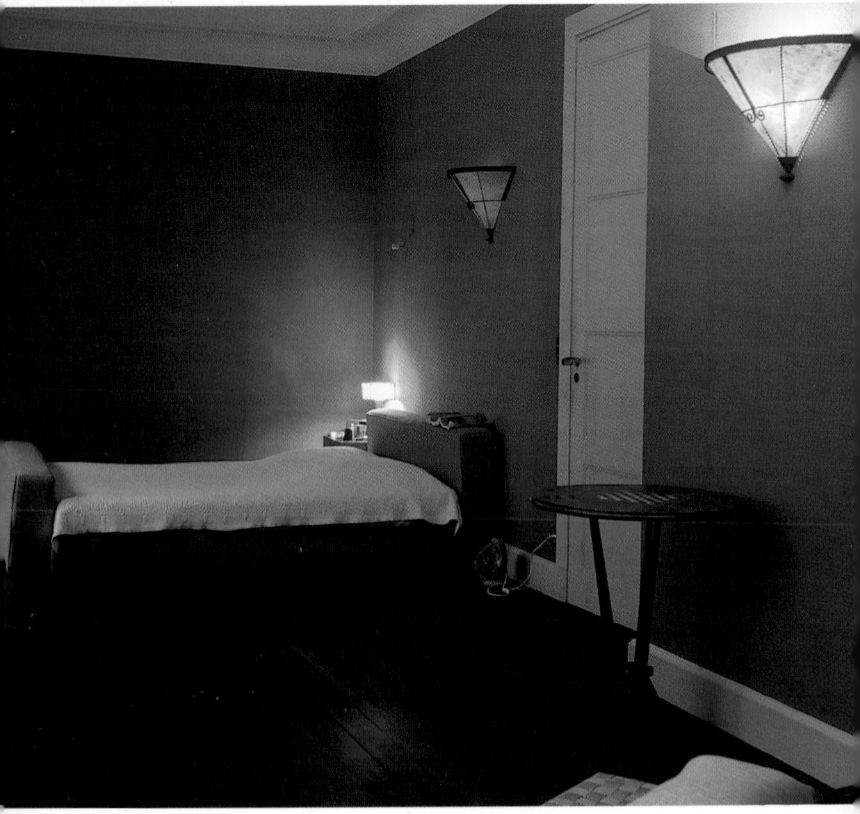

Location: Asnières
Decoration: Pierre Hermé
Photos: © Roland Beaufre (Agence Top)
Fax: +33 1 45 74 20 10

Gourmet Design

The house of the renown French dessert chef Pierre Hermé is a mélange of style, form and color that becomes a sort of mini museum of contemporary furniture and objects from the most prominent designers and artists of the 20th century. His postmodern vision within his profession also translates into the decoration of his home. Lamps, chairs, tables, and paintings materialize names such as Starck, Cassina, Charles Eames and Jacobsen. An open living space permits areas that flow into one another. Skylights, windows and white walls bathe the interiors with light, putting on display the eclectic collection of furniture. This decorative assortment evokes neither clutter nor heaviness, and rather a discerning assortment of subtle tastes and details.

Das Zuhause des Konditors und Dessert-Chefs Pierre Hermé ist aufgrund der stilistischen, formalen und farblichen Mischung fast ein kleines Museum für zeitgenössisches Mobiliar und Werke der bedeutensten Künstler des 20. Jahrhunderts. Seine postmoderne Orientierung spiegelt sich in der Inneneinrichtung wieder: Lampen, Stühle, Tische und Bilder von Starck, Cassina, Charles Eames und Jacobson. Ein offenes Wohnzimmer verbindet die übrigen Räume. Oberlichter, Fenster und weiße Wände tauchen die Wohnung in Tageslicht, das das Mobiliar hervorhebt. Diese Stil-Mischung bietet Einblick in den exquisiten Geschmack und die Liebe zum Detail des Besitzers.

Gourmet Design
Pierre Hermé

L'appartement du célèbre créateur-pâtissier Pierre Hermé mélange styles, formes et couleurs et se convertit en musée de pièces de mobilier contemporain et d'objets des artistes phares du XXème siècle. Sa vision professionnelle postmoderne se reflète dans la décoration de son intérieur. Lampes, chaises, tables et peintures de créateurs comme Starck, Cassina, Charles Eames et Jacobsen habillent les espaces essentiels. Un salon ouvert connecte les diverses pièces. Claires-voies, fenêtres et murs blancs baignent l'intérieur de lumière naturelle, soulignant l'importance du mobilier. Ce mélange de styles communique les goûts et le sens du détail du propriétaire.

El apartamento del conocido pastelero francés Pierre Hermé es una mezcla de estilo, forma y color que se convierte en una especie de mini museo de piezas de mobiliario contemporáneo y de objetos de los artistas más relevantes del siglo XX. Su visión posmoderna de su profesión se refleja en la decoración de los interiores. Lámparas, sillas, mesas y pinturas de autores como Starck, Cassina, Charles Eames y Jacobsen llenan los espacios más importantes del interior. Un salón muy abierto permite conectar las distintas estancias. Claraboyas, ventanas y las paredes en blanco bañan de luz natural el interior, resaltando la importancia del mobiliario. Esta mezcla de estilos evidencia los gustos y el placer por los detalles del propietario.

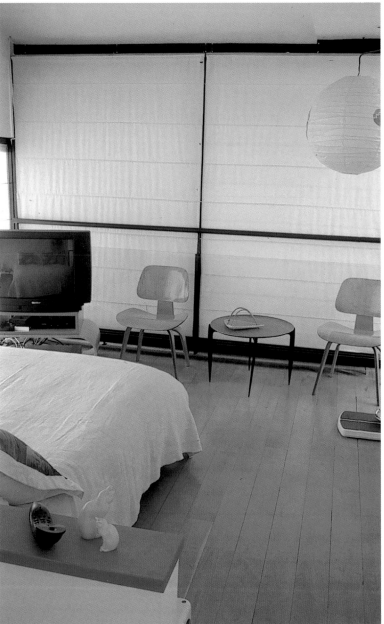

Location: Paris
Architect: Iwan Chavanne
Photos: © Olivier Hallot

A Wooden Empire

A former studio was transformed into an apartment organized on three levels. The living room was situated on the main floor, the bedroom in the basement, and the dining room on the first floor. To unify these volumes, Iwan Chavanne decided to finish the walls in Chablis, a name known for its reference to the wines of Bourgogne, but here the name was given to these planks of pine from Megéve. Their natural clarity gives the rooms tranquility, emphasizing the furniture and objects. In the living room, the cathedral effect granted by the height of the ceilings is accentuated by the wooden blinds made of American linen that cover the windows. These are found in other rooms, evoking colonial references and unifying the entire space.

Dieses aus einer ehemaligen Werkstatt entstandene Apartment ist auf drei Ebenen angelegt: das Wohnzimmer im Erdgeschoss, der Essbereich im ersten Stock und die übrigen Räume im Souterrain. Zur einheitlichen Gestaltung verkleidete Iwan Chavanne sämtliche Wände mit Holzplanken "Chablis" aus Megéve-Tanne, die normalerweise zum Bau von Chalets dienen. Die natürliche helle Färbung verleiht den Räumen Ruhe und betont Möbel und Objekte. Im Wohnzimmer wird der durch die Deckenhöhe hervorgerufene Eindruck einer Kathedrale durch die vor dem Fenster angebrachte Lindenholz-Verkleidung noch verstärkt. Sie taucht in den übrigen Zimmern wieder auf und erinnert an kolonialen Baustil.

A Wooden Empire
Iwan Chavanne

Cet ancien atelier transformé en appartement s'organise sur trois niveaux. Séjour au rez de chaussée, chambres en sous-sol et salle à manger à l'étage. Pour unifier ces volumes Iwan Chavanne a choisi d'habiller les murs de Chablis. Cette gouleyante appellation de vins de Bourgogne désigne aussi les planches en sapin de Megéve utilisées pour la construction des chalets. Sa blondeur naturelle nimbe les pièces d'une délicieuse tranquillité et met en valeur les meubles et les objets chinés. Dans le salon l'effet cathédrale apporté par la hauteur sous plafond est accentué par des stores en tilleul d'Amérique adossés à la verrière. On retrouve ces stores en bois dans les autres pièces qui évoquent irrésistiblement les demeures coloniales et soulignent l'unité du lieu.

Este antiguo taller transformado en apartamento se organiza en tres niveles. La sala de estar se encuentra en la planta baja, las habitaciones en el subsuelo, y el comedor en el primer piso. Para unificar estos volúmenes, Iwan Chavanne ha elegido vestir las paredes con "chablis" : planchas de madera de pino de Megéve utilizadas para la construcción. Su color rubio natural aporta a las habitaciones una deliciosa tranquilidad y pone de relieve los muebles y objetos decorativos. En el salón, la impresión de catedral creada por la altura de los techos se acentúa con estores de tilo americano adosados a los ventanales. Estos estores vuelven a aparecer en el resto de habitaciones evocando indefectiblemente las viviendas coloniales y unificando el espacio.

Location: 11ème Arrondissement
Architect: Marc Hertrich
Photos: © Olivier Hallot
contact@marchertrich.com

Modern Orientalism

This apartment is a laboratory of ideas. Passionate for both color and texture, Marc Hertrich's work lies in playing with the old and the new—loaded Byzantine wallpaper, Turkish tapestries, silk cushions and contemporary lighting. The important thing is to confront materials, combine things we like, and offer a second life to eclectic objects. This is translated into sensual rooms filled with objects, and other more simple rooms, nearly empty, that convey a breath of fresh air. The apartment is centered around three very colorful and transitted rooms: the kitchen, dining and living room, which lead to a purified bedroom painted in black, adorned with a great white porthole and white bathroom that evokes the 1930's. The ensemble creates a poetic living space tinted with orientalism.

Dieses Apartment ist ein Labor der Ideen. Farben und Texturen sind die Leidenschaft des Innenarchitekten. Sein Hobby ist das Spiel mit dem Antiken und dem Modernen, mit überladenen byzantinischen Tapeten, türkischen Wandteppichen, Seidenkissen und modernen Lampen. Das drückt sich in übervollen, sehr gemütlichen und fast leeren, entspannenden Räumen aus. Das Apartment gruppiert sich um drei extrem farbenfrohe Räume: Küche, Esszimmer und Wohnzimmer, die auf ein schwarzgestrichenes Schlafzimmer mit einem riesengroßen weißen Rundfenster und ein weißes Bad gehen, das an die 30er Jahre erinnert. Dieses Ensemble schafft einen poetischen Lebensraum mit orientalischem Flair.

Modern Orientalism
Marc Hertrich

Cet appartment est un véritable laboratoire à idées. L'architect aime jouer avec l'ancien et le neuf, les lourdes tentures viscontiennes, les tapis turcs, les coussins de soie et les luminaires contemporains. L'important est de confronter des matières, de mélanger des chose que l'on aime, et de donner une second vie à des objets éclectiques. Cela se traduit par des piéces trés remplies, très chaleureuses et d'autres très simples, presque vides, des aires de repos. L'appartement s'articule autour de trois pièces très colorées qui aboutissent sur une chambre épurée peinte en noire, omée d'un immenses oeil de boef blanc, et sur une salle de bain blanche qui évoque les années 30. Le tout donne un lieu de vie très poétique teinté d'orientalisme.

Este apartamento es un laboratorio de ideas. Le gusta por encima de todo jugar con lo antiguo y lo nuevo, los pesados cortinajes viscontinos, los tapices turcos, los cojines de seda y las lámparas contemporáneas. Lo importante es confrontar materias, mezclar elementos que nos gusten, y dar una segunda vida a objetos eclécticos. Este planteamiento se traduce en habitaciones muy llenas, muy cálidas y otras, casi vacías, que invitan al reposo. El apartamento se articula alrededor de tres ámbitos muy coloristas, la cocina, el comedor y el salón, que conducen a una habitación pintada de negro, decorada con un inmenso ojo de buey blanco, y a un baño también blanco que evoca los años 30. El conjunto logra un espacio muy poético teñido de orientalismo.

Location: 10ème Arrondissement
Interior Designer: Marie-France de Saint-Félix
Photos: © Olivier Hallot
dsfcrea@aol.com

La Gelta

For the tuaregs of the desert, "Gelta" signifies a place in the desert where water surges from a spring and returns to the sand. Marie-France de Saint-Félix, who has always venerated the purity of a space, was inspired by this asthetic place in realizing this apartment. Here, as in the desert, the colors of the sand devour the space and suddenly we are taken by surprise at the sound of water from a fountain. The liquid actually has the illusion of disappearing under a mysterious vault. This place was conceived solely to alleviate a very hectic lifestyle. There is a continuous access between the bedroom and the pool, passing through a small arched living room. The floors, walls and ceilings were realized with river sand, limestone, white cement, and dirt from the ocre land of Roussillon, which gives them thickness.

Für die Tuaregs bedeutet "Gelta" ein Ort in der Wüste, wo Wasser aus einer Quelle sprudelt und zum Sand zurückkehrt. Das Design für diesen Innenraum wurde von jenem asketischen Ort inspiriert. Auch hier verschlingen die Farben des Sandes den Raum, und überrascht hören wir plötzlich das Plätschern einer Quelle, deren Wasser unter einem geheimnisvollen Gewölbe zu verschwinden scheint. Nicht einmal ein Telefon gibt es in dieser vollkommenen Isolierung. Zwischen Springbrunnen und Zimmer geht man durch ein kleines gewölbtes Wohnzimmer. Fußböden, Wände und Decken wurden mit Flusssand, Kalk, weißem Zement und ockerfarbenem Sand aus dem Roussillon ausgeführt.

La Gelta
Marie-France de Saint-Félix

Pour les Touaregs "Gelta" est un endroit dans le désert où l'eau jaillit d'une source et repart dans le sable. Marie-France de Saint-Félix qui a toujours célébré le lieux épurés s'est inspirée de ce lieu ascétique pour réaliser cet appartement. Ici, comme dans le désert, les couleurs du sable dévorent l'espace; et, tout à coup on est stupéfait d'entendre l'eau s'écouler dans un bassin. Le liquide semble même s'enfuir sous un voûte mystérieuse. Ce lieu a été uniquement conçu pour marquer des pauses dans une vie trés occupée. On circule librement du bassin à la chambre en passant par un petit salon voûté. Les sols, les murs et les plafonds ont été réalisés à partir de sable de rivière, de la chaux, du ciment blanc et de la terre ocre du Roussillon.

Para los tuaregs "Gelta" es un lugar del desierto donde el agua mana de una fuente y vuelve a la arena. Marie-France de Saint-Félix se inspiró en este lugar ascético para diseñar este interior. Aquí, como en el desierto, los colores de la arena devoran el espacio; y de repente nos sorprende oír el agua de una fuente. El líquido parece incluso, por un efecto visual, escaparse bajo una bóveda misteriosa. No hay teléfono, de manera que el aislamiento puede ser total. De la fuente a la habitación se circula libremente pasando por un pequeño salón abovedado. Todos los volúmenes se han tratado sin cambiar los materiales. Los suelos, las paredes y los techos se han realizado a partir de arena de río, cal, cemento blanco y tierra ocre del Rosellón, que les confiere espesor.

Location: 16ème Arrondissement
Architect: Jean-Jacques Ory
Photos: © Olivier Hallot
jeanjacques-ory@worldonline.fr

Sculptural Fireplace

In an austere building from 1925, the architect has achieved a modern realization; dilating a 200 m² space by playing with space, light and metal. The first step was to tear down the conglomeration of rooms with moldings, the parquet and old chimneys and then the false ceilings. The living room has a height of 10 meters. In this vertical space, a monumental chimney made from curved hammered steel evokes an airliner's cockpit. Closeby, a micro-perforated steel library acts as both a wall and a metallic staircase. This open area faces the dining room and a stainless steel kitchen. The originality of the space is reinstated by the discontinuity of the floor made of polished and tinted concrete, interrupted by an exotic wooden rug.

In einem schlichten Gebäude von 1925 hat der Architekt die vorhandenen 200 m² durch den spielerischen Umgang mit Raum, Licht und Metall erweitert. Wand- und Deckenverkleidung sowie die alten Kamine wurden entfernt. Das Wohnzimmer hat 10 m hohe Decken, an einer Seite befindet sich ein geschwungener Kamin aus gehämmertem Stahl, der an einen Flugzeugrumpf erinnert. Daneben dient ein Bücherregal aus Lochblech zugleich als Wand und Treppe. Dieser offene Bereich führt zur Essecke und der Küche aus Edelstahl. Die Originalität der Wohnung wird durch den abwechslungsreich gestalteten Boden betont: polierter und gefärbter Beton, unterbrochen durch exotisches Holz.

Sculptural Fireplace
Jean-Jacques Ory

Dans un sobre immeuble 1925, l'architecte a réussi un exercice moderne, dilater un lieu de 200 m² en jouant avec l'espace, la lumière et la métal. Il a fallu casser cet enchevêtrement de pièces avec moulures, parquet et vieilles cheminées. Les combes ont été éliminées. Le séjour bénéficie d'une hauteur sous plafond d'une dizaine de mètres. Dans cet espace vertical, une cheminée monumentale en acier martelé, galbé, évoque la carlingue d'une avion. Tout prés une bibliothèque en acier micro perforé sert aussi de pario et d'un escalier en métal. Cette zone ouverte donne sur une salle à manger et un cuisine en inox. L'originalité du lieu est soulignée par la non continuité du sol, de béton teinté et poli, interrompu par un tapis de bois exotique.

En un sobrio edificio de 1925, el arquitecto ha conseguido dilatar un lugar de 200 m² jugando con el espacio, la luz y el metal y haciendo desaparecer la antigua distribución. Para incrementar la sensación de espacio y dejar las vigas a la vista se eliminaron los falsos techos. El salón tiene ahora una altura de diez metros. En este espacio vertical, una chimenea de acero martilleado y curvado evoca la carlinga de un avión. A poca distancia, una biblioteca de acero microperforado sirve de pared y escalera. Esta zona abierta da al comedor y a una cocina de acero inoxidable. La originalidad del lugar se acentúa por la discontinuidad de un suelo de hormigón teñido y pulido, interrumpido por otro de madera exótica.

Location: 9ème Arrondissement
Architect: Alain Salomon
Photos: © Chris Tubbs, Gilles Trillard, Alain Salomon
apsalomon@wanadoo.fr

Interior Garden

This 300 m² loft is located in a small alley close to the Stalingrad Plaza, northeast of Paris, in the middle of a 19th century industrial complex. For this reason, the architect decided to create an interior passage that would protect it from its aggressive surroundings. The original structure belonged to a electric motor repair shop. Now, in the rear a spiral staircase opens up a skylight that illuminates the gallery that looks out onto the dining room. The ground floor, previously the garage, is now a library, a guestroom and a bathroom with sauna. A kitchen articulates the entrance, living room, dining room and gallery. The bedrooms are situated on the second floor.

Dieser 300 m² große Loft befindet sich im Pariser Nordosten in einer kleinen Seitenstraße nahe der Place de Stalingrad. Da der Bau, der zu einem Elektromotorenwerk gehörte, mitten in einem ehemaligen Industriegebiet liegt, wurde eine Landschaft im Inneren geschaffen, die vor der Aggressivität der Umgebung schützen soll. Im hinteren Teil führt eine Wendeltreppe in einen Lichtschacht, der die in den Essbereich mündende Galerie erhellt. Im Erdgeschoss befinden sich anstelle der Garage die Bibliothek, ein Gästezimmer und ein Bad mit Sauna. Die Küche gliedert Eingangs-, Essbereich, Wohnzimmer und Galerie. Die übrigen Zimmer liegen im zweiten Stock.

Interior Garden
Alain Salomon

Ce loft de 300 m² habite une ruelle proche de la place Stalingrad, le Nord-Est parisien, au cœur d'un complexe industriel XIX°. De ce fait un paysage intérieur fut projeté, protégeant de l'agressivité ambiante. À l'arrière de la structure originelle, un ancien atelier de moteurs électriques, se trouve un escalier en colimaçon donnant sur un puits de lumière et inondant de lumière la galerie débouchant sur la salle à manger. En bas, l'ancien garage accueille la bibliothèque, une chambre d'hôte et un bain avec sauna. Une cuisine articule l'entrée, le salon/salle à manger et la galerie. Les chambres occupent le deuxième étage.

Este loft, de 300 m² está situado en un pequeño callejón cercano a la plaza de Stalingrad, al nordeste de París, en medio de un complejo industrial del siglo XIX. Por este motivo, se decidió crear un paisaje interior que protegiera de las antiestéticas vistas del entorno. La estructura original perteneció a un taller de motores eléctricos. Ahora, en la parte trasera se sitúa una escalera de caracol cuya cubierta permite el paso de la luz para iluminar la galería que desemboca en el comedor. En la planta baja, donde antes estaba el garaje, se encuentra ahora la entrada, una cocina, el salón, el comedor, la biblioteca, el cuarto de invitados, la galería y un baño con sauna. Las habitaciones se ubican en el segundo piso.

Location: 10ème Arrondissement
Architect: Francesco Passanitti
Photos: © Olivier Hallot
passabf@hotmail.com

Rue de la Grange Aux Belles

This small apartment has proved to be a great accomplishment by the Italian architect who finished it entirely in concrete. The result: a modern and functional space that metamorphosizes according to the tastes and needs of its journalist tenant. A studio and meeting place during the day transforms into luxurious bedroom at night. The bedroom disposes of a unique bed structure that ascends and disappears to make room for an office desk. The dining corner integrates itself at an angle composed by an almond-colored polished concrete shelf and a panelled concrete wall adorned with artificial fossils. In the kitchen the marble sink combines with a yellow concrete worktop. The red and black concrete inside the Japanese-style bathroom was treated to look like stonework.

Dieses kleine Apartment bot dem italienischen Architekten einen fantastischen Rahmen für eine Betonverkleidung vom Boden bis zur Decke. Das Ergebnis: eine moderne und funktionale Wohnung nach dem Geschmack ihrer Bewohnerin, einer Journalistin. Tagsüber ein Büro und über Nacht ein luxuriöses Schlafzimmer. Das Bett wird hochgezogen, verschwindet und macht dem Schreibtisch Platz. In einer Ecke, die aus einem mandelfarbenen Betonregal und einer Wand aus Betonpaneelen gebildet wird, befindet sich das Esszimmer. In der Küche harmonieren Marmorbecken und Arbeitstisch aus gelbem Beton. Das Bad im japanischen Stil mit rotem und schwarzen Beton erinnert an Steinwerk.

Rue de la Grange Aux Belles

Francesco Passanitti

Ce petit appartement a servi de cadre fantaisiste pour cet architecte italien qui l'a habillé de béton, du sol au plafond. Résultat : un lieu moderne et fonctionnel. L'intégralité de l'endroit se métamorphose au gré des envies de son occupante, une journaliste. D'un lieu d'écriture ou de réunion le jour, cet espace se transforme en une luxueuse chambre la nuit. Cette dernière est dotée d'un lit ascenseur, qui disparaît pour laisser la place au bureau. Le coin salle à manger s'insère dans un angle composé d'une étagère en béton teinté et poli couleur amande et une paroi de plusieurs panneaux de béton faussement fossilisés. Dans la cuisine, l'évier en mar-bre se marie au plan de travail en béton en terrazzo jaune paille. Dans la salle de bain japonisante, le béton a été travaillé comme de la pierre, en rouge et noir.

Este pequeño apartamento ha servido de fantástico marco para el arquitecto italiano, que lo ha vestido de hormigón desde el suelo hasta el techo. Resultado: un lugar moderno y funcional. El lugar se metamorfosea íntegro a gusto de su ocupante, una periodista. De lugar de escritura durante el día, el espacio se transforma en un lujoso dormitorio de noche. Este último contiene una cama ascensor que desaparece para ceder el espacio al escritorio. El comedor se integra en un ángulo compuesto por una estantería de hormigón teñido y pulido color almendra y una pared de varios paneles de hormigón. En la cocina, se combinan el mármol del fregadero y el hormigón amarillo de la mesa de trabajo. En el baño, de estilo japonés, el hormigón ha sido trabajado como piedra, en rojo y negro.

Location: Paris
Architect: François Murracciole
Photos: © Morel M. Pierre
francois.murracciole@libertysurf.fr

Light

The project consisted in converting the space into a comfortable and luminous home that would take advantage of the elements that would maintain the original character of the studio which it had once been. The patio, found in the center of the space, had been concealed by a plastic ceiling; tearing it down brought with it an abundance of light that reached even the bedroom located in the former warehouse. Next to the windows that face the patio, an attic serves as a guest or TV room. Opening the patio in summer transforms the living room into an exterior lounge area.

Der Entwurf hatte die Schaffung einer komfortablen lichten Wohnfläche unter Beibehaltung der originalen Elemente der zuvor hier untergebrachten Werkstatt zum Ziel. Nach Abriss der Plastikdecke, die den zentralen Hof verbarg, flutet Licht durch alle Räume bis hinein in die Zimmer des ehemaligen Lagers. Neben dem großen Fenster zum Hof liegt eine Dachstube, die sowohl für Gäste als auch als Fernsehzimmer benutzt wird. Im Sommer, wenn die Tür zum Hof geöffnet wird, verwandelt sich das Wohnzimmer in einen Raum im Freien.

Light
François Murracciole

Le projet avait pour objectif de convertir le lieu en un espace confortable et lumineux, pour vivre et profiter des éléments préservant la personnalité originelle de l'ancien atelier. Le patio, au cœur de l'espace, était caché par un toit de plastique. Sa démolition a permis de diffuser la lumière dans l'ensemble des pièces, même dans les chambres situées dans l'ancien magasin. Près de la baie du patio, une mezzanine s'habille en chambre d'hôte ou en salle de télévision. En été, l'ouverture du patio transforme le salon en une salle à l'air libre.

El proyecto consistía en convertir el lugar en un espacio confortable y luminoso en el cual se pudiera vivir y aprovechar los elementos que mantuvieran el carácter original del taller que había albergado. El patio, situado en el centro del espacio, estaba oculto por un techo de plástico cuyo derribo consiguió hacer llegar la luz a todos los ambientes, incluidas las habitaciones ubicadas en el antiguo almacén. Junto al ventanal que da al patio, hay un altillo que hace las veces de habitación de huéspedes o de sala de televisión. Al abrir el patio en el verano, el salón se transforma en una sala al aire libre.

Location: 6ème Arrondissement
Architect: Stéphane Chamard
Photos: © Vincent Leroux

Functional Forms

At the far end of a patio in the 6th district of Paris, a 16 m² space used by the concierge of the building was transformed by the young architect Stéphane Chamard into a luminous working and living space. This cubic volume possessed a great height that permitted the structure to be designed on two levels, in which every centimeter was calculated with the aim of putting the space and its large windows to use in the best way possible. The original design of the staircase near the entrance is one of the attractive features of this small and functional apartment.

Am hinteren Ende eines Innenhofes im 6ème Arrondissement von Paris befand sich diese Hausmeisterloge von 16 m² Größe, die der junge Architekt Stéphane Chamard in einen hellen Lebens- und Arbeitsraum verwandelt hat. Der rechteckige Raum hat besonders hohe Decken, was die Möglichkeit bot, ihn auf zwei Ebenen anzulegen. Dabei wurde jeder Zentimeter so berechnet, dass der vorhandene Raum sowie die hohen Fenster optimal genutzt werden und funktionalen Ansprüchen genügen. Eine nahe dem Eingang gelegene Treppe besticht durch ihr außergewöhnliches Design.

Functional Forms
Stéphane Chamard

Le fond d'un patio du 6° arrondissement abrite cet espace de 16 m², destiné au concierge de la résidence et transformé par le jeune architecte Stéphane Chamard en un lumineux intérieur, de vie et de travail. Le volume cubique tout en hauteur a permis la conception d'une structure sur deux niveaux, où chaque centimètre est calculé pour jouir de l'espace et des baies, l'appartement acquérant ainsi un caractère fonctionnel. Un escalier face à l'entrée est souligné par l'originalité de son design.

Al fondo de un patio del distrito 6 de París se encontraba este espacio de 16 m² destinado al conserje de la finca, y que el joven arquitecto Stéphane Chamard ha transformado en un luminoso interior para vivir y trabajar. Se trata de un volumen de forma cúbica de gran altura que ha permitido diseñar una estructura en dos niveles, en donde se ha calculado cada centímetro con el fin de aprovechar el espacio y los ventanales, y dotar así al apartamento de un carácter funcional. Una escalera situada frente a la entrada destaca por su original diseño.

Location: 1er Arrondissement
Interior Designer: Masakasu Bokura
Photos: © Roland Beaufre (Agence Top)
Fax: +33 1 42 60 08 99

Paris Zen

The owner of this apartment desired a space that would evoke a certain Zen air and still maintain loyalty to its Parisian ground. Masakasu Bokura is known for his luminous, light and spacious creations that eliminate all that is unnecessary. Here, he painted the walls white, laid a light parquet, and employed sliding translucent panels in place of doors. Near the entrance, a high-tech kitchen is an attractive element that leads to the rest of the minimalist space. Hints of color, select furniture and decorative pieces add sophistication to this Parisian residence.

Wunsch des Besitzers war eine vom Zen-Buddhismus inspirierte Wohnung, die dennoch dem Pariser Lebensstil treu bleibt. Masakasu Bokura ist bekannt für seinen erfolgreichen Umgang mit Tageslicht und seine lichtbestimmten Entwürfe, die alles Unnötige vermeiden. Die Wände wurden weiß gestrichen, helles Parkett verlegt und durchscheinende Schiebeelemente, die die Funktion von Türen übernehmen, angebracht. Nahe der Eingangstür befindet sich die Küche in High-Tech-Ästhetik, die in den übrigen, minimalistischen Wohnbereich führt. Farbliche Elemente, ausgewähltes Mobiliar und die außergewöhnliche Dekoration verleihen dieser Pariser Wohnung eine exklusive Note.

Paris Zen
Masakasu Bokura

Le propriétaire désirait un espace évoquant le zen tout en restant fidèle au style de vie parisien. Masakasu Bokura est célèbre pour la réussite de son travail sur la lumière naturelle et ses créations lumineuses, ennemies du superflu. Ici, ont été peints de blanc les murs, installés des parquets aux tons clairs et conçus des panneaux translucides coulissants en sorte de porte. Près de l'entrée, une cuisine high-tech nous mène au reste d'un l'appartement à la distribution très minimaliste. Notes colorées, mobilier choisi et pièces décoratives insolites emplissent de sophistication cette demeure parisienne.

El propietario de este apartamento deseaba un espacio que evocara cierta atmósfera zen, pero manteniéndose leal al estilo de vida de París. Masakasu Bokura es conocido por su exitoso tratamiento de la luz natural y por sus creaciones luminosas que eliminan todo lo innecesario. En este interior, se pintaron las paredes en blanco, se instaló un parqué de tonos claros y se diseñaron unos paneles deslizantes translúcidos a modo de puertas. Cerca de la entrada, una cocina de estética high-tech nos conduce al resto de la estancia, muy minimalista. Notas de color, un selecto mobiliario y piezas decorativas curiosas llenan de sofisticación esta residencia parisiense.

Location: Paris
Architect: Cristina and Alexandre Negoescu
Photos: © Mihail Moldoveanu

Extravagance and Dreams

The architects materialised the owner's longing for an extravagant space where he could enjoy his unusual collection of furniture and objects. The various areas form a bizarre atmosphere spotted with humorous details. Each environment denotes an individual theme that is represented through minute details. The dining room plays on the vibration of reflected images, with its luxurious goldleaf surfaces bouncing light onto the mirror mosaic that coats the walls. The opulent living room evokes an exotic tone and points to a display cabinet brimming with the most curious of objects. The library recreates the atmosphere of a 19th century study hall, while the kitchen explores Pop and 1970's industrial styles.

Die Phantasie der Architekten ermöglichte die Materialisierung der Wünsche des Eigentümers. Die Räume vereinen eine ungewohnte Atmosphäre mit humorvollen Unterbrechungen. Jedes Ambiente unterscheidet sich durch ein besonderes, detailliert dargestelltes Thema: Das Esszimmer spielt mit dem Schillern der Reflektionen. Das Spiegelmosaik an den Wänden mildert den Eindruck der kostbaren vergoldeten Flächen. Im exotischen Wohnraum fällt der Schrank mit den ausgefallensten Gegenständen auf. Die Bibliothek erinnert an die Lesesäle des 19. Jahrhunderts, während die Küche auf Pop und industrielles Designs der 70er Jahre ausgerichtet ist.

Extravagance and Dreams
Cristina and Alexandre Negoescu

Les architectes ont donné corps au désir du propriétaire : un extravagant espace onirique, accueillant meubles et objets rares. Semblant unis par une étrangeté teintée d'humour, les diverses pièces distinguent par des thèmes précis. La salle à manger joue avec la vibration des reflets. Une ambiance féerique, d'inspiration Art Déco, naît de la préciosité des surfaces dorées atténuée par la mosaïque d'éclats de miroir sur les murs. L'envoûtant séjour se teinte d'exotisme, mettant en valeur un cabinet de curiosités. La bibliothèque recrée l'ambiance des salles d'études XIXème et la cuisine explore la couleur et le style propres aux années Pop et à l'industrialisme des années 70.

La imaginación de los arquitectos ha hecho posible materializar el mundo que deseaba el propietario, un apasionado de los muebles insólitos. Los espacios se unen en un ambiente extraño con toques de humor. Cada ambiente se distingue por un tema mostrado con minuciosidad: el comedor juega con la vibración de la imagen reflejada. El preciosismo de las superficies doradas se atenúa con el mosaico de destellos de espejo en las paredes, creando un ambiente mágico que se asemeja al Art Déco. En la sala de estar destaca un armario de curiosidades. La biblioteca recrea la atmósfera de las salas de estudio del siglo XIX, mientras que la cocina explora el ambiente coloreado de los años Pop y del diseño industrial de los 70.

Location: 17ème Arrondissement
Interior Designer: Serge Pons
Photos: © Roland Beaufre (Agence Top)

Antique Austerity

Home to the designer, this Parisian flat surprises with its austere quality and modern features. Located on the seventh floor with views to the Sacred Heart and the Eiffel Tower, this white space is bathed in light and puts on display an impressive collection of sculptures and antiques, each of them thoughtfully placed and lit. Ultra-modern furniture with straight and pure lines like those in the living room, coexist with antique pieces such as the elegant wood bureaus against the wall. While white was chosen for the walls, a grey-green carpet was laid on the floors, creating an elegant base for the chosen furniture. Serge Pons also suggests a play between columns, both structural and freestanding that add to the linear character of the space.

Dieses Apartment eines Designers überrascht durch seine nüchterne und moderne Gestaltung. Im siebten Stock mit Blick auf Sacre Coeur und den Eiffelturm gelegen, präsentiert diese helle und vom Tageslicht durchflutete Wohnung eine beeindruckende und perfekt angeordnete Sammlung von Skulpturen und Antiquitäten. Hochmoderne Designermöbel und klare Linien harmonieren mit altem Mobiliar; dies illustriert die Kommode im Wohnzimmer. Die Wände wurden in Weiß gehalten, während der Boden mit Teppich in Grün- und Grautönen ausgelegt ist. Serge Pons setzt ferner tragende und freistehende Säulen spielerisch ein, die dieser Wohnung Charakter geben.

Antique Austerity
Serge Pons

Accueillant un créateur, cet appartement parisien surprend par sa qualité austère et son design moderne. Septième étage avec vue sur le Sacré Cœur et la Tour Eiffel, cet espace blanc baigné de lumière naturelle affiche avec goût une impressionnante collection de sculptures et d'antiquités. Mobilier ultra moderne et lignes pures, ainsi dans le salon, coexistent avec des pièces anciennes tel le secrétaire en bois appuyé contre un mur. Le blanc habille les parois, comme le tapis vert et gris revêt le sol. Serge Pons suggère un jeu structurel avec les colonnes, conférant une personnalité à l'espace.

Vivienda de un diseñador, este apartamento de París sorprende por su austera calidad y su moderno diseño. Situado en un séptimo piso con vistas a la Iglesia del Sagrado Corazón y a la Torre Eiffel, este espacio en blanco, bañado de luz natural, muestra una impresionante colección de escultura y antigüedades perfectamente expuesta. Mobiliario de diseño ultra moderno y líneas puras como las del salón coexiste con piezas antiguas como la cómoda de madera situada junto a una de las paredes. Se utilizó el blanco para decorar las paredes, así como una alfombra de tonos verdes y grises para el suelo. Serge Pons sugiere asimismo un juego estructural con las columnas, que dan carácter al espacio.

Location: St. Cloud
Architect: Annie Verlant
Photos: © Olivier Hallot
gverlant@bygcollector.com

Fusion of Style

The objective of interior architect Annie Verlant was to give charm to an uninteresting 19th century house. In order to do this, she added mouldings and introduced an antique red-lacquered bathtub. A sculptural central double door closes off the bathroom. Its yellow and white aged gold tones strengthen the luminosity of the bedroom. To create both a rustic and refined style in the bedroom, parquet accompanies an antique bed with wooden posts adorned with braided tassles. In the living room, African art is on display, along with natural materials, such as the linen sofa, oxidated metal tables and a fiber rug.

Die Innenarchitektin Annie Verlant wollte einem relativ uninteressanten Haus aus dem 19. Jahrhundert zu Charme verhelfen. Dazu fügte sie Simse hinzu und installierte eine alte, rotlackierte Badewanne. Eine neue zentrale Doppeltür lässt die ursprüngliche zu einem reinen Dekor werden. Gelb- und Weißtöne zusammen mit Altgold geben dem Schlafraum mehr Licht. Ein antikes Bett mit Holzsäulen und Bortenschmuck vermittelt zusammen mit dem Parkett einen zugleich rustikalen und doch eleganten Eindruck. Im Wohnzimmer wird afrikanische Kunst mit einem Leinensofa, kleinen rostüberzogenen Metalltischen und einem Sisalteppich kombiniert.

Fusion of Style
Annie Verlant

Donner un charme à une maison du XIXe siècle qui n'en avait pas, tel a été l'objectif de l'architecte d'intérieur Annie Verlant. Pour cela elle a rajouté des moulures, chinée une baignoire ancienne que'elle a habillé de laque rouge. Aujourd'hui, une porte centrale à double battant s'ouvre sur cette dernière qui devient sculpturale. La chambre este rendue plus lumineuese par des tonlités jaunes et blanches ponctuées accueille un lit ancien à colonnes en bois, habillé e passementeries. Dans le salon l'art africain est mis en valeur par des matériaux naturels, tels qu'un canapé en lin, des tables basses en métal rouillé, un tapis en sisal.

El objetivo de la arquitecta interiorista Annie Verlant era dar encanto a una desangelada casa del siglo XIX. Para ello se pusieron molduras y se instaló una bañera antigua que se revistió de laca roja. Una nueva puerta central de doble batiente convierte a la original en meramente escultórica. Las tonalidades amarillas y blancas con oro viejo aportan más luminosidad a la habitación, en la que sobre el parqué despejado se ha dispuesto una cama antigua con columnas de madera, vestidas con pasamanería. En el salón, el arte africano se combina con materiales naturales, un sofá de lino, mesillas de metal oxidado y una alfombra de sisal.

Location: 15ème Arrondissement
Photos: © Roland Beaufre (Agence Top)

Becoming a Loft

This apartment was reformed by its tenants with the aid of an architect friend. The 250 m² space was transformed into an open loft space by eliminating walls, removing carpets and painting walls white. The kitchen, dining and living room share a 60 m² space that continue toward an exterior private terrace. The bedroom is partitioned off for privacy and interacts with a small studio space with a desk and book shelf. Contemporary furniture and simple lines mingle with flower vases, sculptures and curious lamps to form an interesting, modern and practical home.

Dieses Apartment wurde von den Besitzern mit Hilfe eines befreundeten Architekten umgestaltet. Die 250 m² Wohnung wurde entkernt, Teppiche und Auslegware verlegt und die Wände weiß gestrichen. Küche, Essbereich und Wohnzimmer nehmen eine Fläche von 60 m² ein, die durch eine Außenterrasse fortgesetzt wird. Um eine private Atmosphäre zu schaffen, wurde das Schlafzimmer vom Rest der Wohnung abgetrennt. Es dient gleichzeitig als kleines Studio mit elegantem Glastisch und Bücherschrank. Zeitgenössisches Mobiliar und einfache Linien mischen sich mit farbenfrohen Vasen, Skulpturen und kurios gestalteten Lampen und schaffen so eine moderne und praktische Atmosphäre.

Becoming a Loft

Rénové par les proprietaires avec l'aide d'un ami architecte, l'espace de 250 m² est devenu diaphane en éliminant les partitions divisant les diverses pièces. Tapis et moquette furent ajoutés et les murs peints en blanc. Cuisine, salle à manger et séjour partagent une surface de 60 m² se prolongeant par une terrasse extérieure privative. La chambre est séparée des autres espaces, pour l'intimité, devenant un studio avec table et bibliothèque. Le mobilier contemporain aux lignes simples se marie aux vases colorés, sculptures et lampes aux curieuses formes pour former un intérieur moderne et pratique.

Este apartamento fue reformado por sus habitantes con la ayuda de un amigo arquitecto. El espacio original de 250 m² fue transformado en diáfano tras la eliminación de una serie de particiones que dividían distintas habitaciones. Se añadieron moquetas y alfombras y se pintaron las paredes de blanco. La cocina, el comedor y la sala de estar comparten un área de 60 m², que continúa con una zona de terraza privada exterior. El dormitorio, separado del resto de los espacios para dotarlo de privacidad, hace las veces asimismo de pequeño estudio con mesa y librería. Un mobiliario de estilo contemporáneo y líneas sencillas se mezcla con jarrones coloristas, esculturas y lámpara de formas curiosas para conformar un interior moderno y práctico.

Location: 7ème Arrondissement
Interior Designer: Catherine Memmi
Photos: © Roland Beaufre (Agence Top)
Fax: +33 1 45 44 99 69

Chic Antique

The project of this apartment bases itself on order, rationality and austerity as the most noticeable characteristics. The space has been treated as a large and neutral container in which luminosity and the purity of white unify the natural materials like wood or marble, converting them into the main feature of the space. The absence of excess elements such as the special disposition and division of areas creates open, suggestive, and personal spaces that fluctuate between an avant-garde and classical aesthetic demonstrated by the absence of color and any sort of gaudiness. A home with a unique style in which the furniture and ornamental objects take care of offering that particular atmosphere which it breathes.

Der Entwurf für diese Wohnung beruht auf Ordnung, Zweckmäßigkeit und Einfachheit als auffälligsten Kennzeichen. Man hat den vorhandenen großen und neutralen Raum so gestaltet, dass Tageslicht und reines Weiß in Verbindung mit edlen Materialen wie Holz und Marmor besonders zur Geltung kommen. Die Abwesenheit von überflüssigen Elementen sowie die besondere Anordnung und Struktur der einzelnen Bereiche bilden offene, anregende und sehr persönliche Räume. Ihr Stil – zwischen avantgardistischer Ästhetik und klassizistischer Gestaltung – wird durch die Abwesenheit von Farben und schrillen Elementen noch verstärkt.

Chic Antique
Catherine Memmi

Ce projet repose sur l'ordre, la rationalité et l'austérité, en préceptes primordiaux. L'espace a été distribué en figurant un grand conteneur où la luminosité et la pureté du blanc unies aux matériaux nobles, bois ou marbre, acquièrent une présence singulière. L'absence d'éléments superflus, comme la disposition spéciale et l'organisation des ambiances créent des intérieurs ouverts, suggestifs et personnels, d'une esthétique avant-gardiste à un exquis classicisme stimulés par l'absence de couleur et de tons criards. Un espace au style propre où mobilier et ornements, choisis avec un bon sens inhabituel, engendrent l'atmosphère singulière émanant du lieu.

El proyecto de este apartamento se basa en el orden, la racionalidad y la austeridad como premisas más destacables. Se ha solucionado el espacio como si se tratara de un gran contenedor neutro en el que la luminosidad y pureza del blanco, unida a los materiales nobles como la madera o el mármol, adquiere un singular protagonismo. La ausencia de elementos superfluos, así como la especial disposición y organización de los ambientes, configuran unos interiores abiertos, sugestivos y muy personales que cabalgan entre una estética vanguardista y unos exquisitos aires clásicos potenciados por la ausencia de color y estridencias. Un espacio con estilo propio en el que el mobiliario y los objetos ornamentales se encargan de ofrecer esa particular atmósfera que respira el ambiente.

Location: 10ème Arrondissement
Architect: Gilles Bouchez
Photos: © Olivier Hallot
Tel.: +33 1 42 39 44 39

Place de la République

This building from 1920 is located among the gardens of a 18th century mansion catalogued as a Historical Monument. A 3.10 meter glazed door leads inside the apartment and faces a staircase adorned by a luminous sculpture. From the threshold an important view can be had of the living room that measures 18.5 meters in length up to the bedroom. The architect opened up unused studio spaces to recompose the space's initial U-shaped plan. Parquet made from dark Jatoba wood from Amazonia unifies the whole area. A staircase that doubles as storage was placed in the kitchen and leads to the roof terrace with views of the Sacred Heart.

Dieses Gebäude von 1920 liegt in den Gärten einer Villa aus dem 18. Jahrhundert und steht unter Denkmalschutz. Die 3,10 m hohe verglaste Eingangstür führt zu einer mit einer Skulptur dekorierten Treppe. Von der Schwelle aus sieht man das 18,5 m lange Wohnzimmer bis hin zum Schlafzimmer. Dazu hat der Architekt alte Studioräume zur Wiederherstellung der ursprünglichen U-Struktur genutzt. Parkett aus dunklem Jatoba vereinheitlicht den gesamten Raum. Ein Treppenmöbel in der Küche führt auf das Dach zur Gartenterrasse mit Blick auf Sacré Coeur.

Place de la République
Gilles Bouchez

Cet immeuble de 1920 est situé dans les jardins d'un hôtel particulier du XVIIIe siècle répertorié dans l'inventaire des Monuments Historiques. On pénètre dans l'appartement par un porte vitrée de 3,10 mètres de haut, qui invite à gravir un escalier orné d'une sculpture lumineuese. Le seuil offre une vue d'angle très importante qui parcourt le salon de 18,50 mètre de long jusque dans la chambre. Pour cela l'architecte a du dégagé des ateliers de confection cloisonnés pour recomposer la structure en "U" initiale. Un parquet en Jatobe, un bois sombre d'Amazonie, souligne l'unité du lieu. Un meuble escalier insère la cuisine et mène sur le toit où au jardin terrasse regarde vers le Sacré Coeur.

Este edificio de 1920 está situado en los jardines de una mansión del siglo XVIII, catalogada como Monumento Histórico. Se accede al apartamento por una puerta vidriada de 3,10 metros de alto, que invita a subir una escalera decorada con una escultura. El umbral ofrece una vista de ángulo que recorre el salón de 18,5 metros de largo hasta el dormitorio. Para ello, el arquitecto ha tenido que aprovechar los antiguos talleres de confección para recomponer la estructura en "U" original. Un parqué de jatoba subraya la unidad del lugar. Un mueble escalera integra la cocina y lleva a la cubierta, donde un jardín-terraza se orienta hacia el Sagrado Corazón.

Location: 14ème Arrondissement
Architect: Littow Architects
Photos: © Pekka Littow
littow@magic.fr

Penthouse Ave du Maine

This apartment is arranged through separate free-standing pieces that each contribute a sense of boundary and color to the space. These separate linear and cubic volumes take the form of a fireplace, a bookcase and a kitchen unit. The kitchen and dining area is separated by the light blue book shelf that occupies most of the apartment´s width. Here a fireplace is integrated into a partition of the same color. In the kitchen a pistacho green kitchen island divides the cooking and eating space. Wooden beams were left exposed and painted white, as were the walls, along which one runs a staircase that leads to the upper level.

Dieses Apartment wird durch voneinander unabhängige Elemente unterteilt, die gleichzeitig den Raum farblich gestalten. Die freistehenden rechteckigen Raumteiler dienen als Kamin, Bücherregal und eine in das Wohnzimmer integrierte Küche, die abgegrenzt durch ein hellblaues Bücherregal, das sich fast über die gesamte Breite des Raumes erstreckt, einen eigenen Bereich bildet. Eine pistazienfarbene Kücheninsel trennt Koch- und Essbereich voneinander. Offenliegende Holzbalken wurden weiß gestrichen, ebenso die Wände; entlang einer dieser Wände führt eine Treppe auf die zweite Ebene.

Penthouse Ave du Maine
Littow Architects

Cet appartement est distribué en pièces libres séparées, délimitant et colorant l'espace. Les différents volumes linéaires et cubiques deviennent une cheminée, une bibliothèque et une cuisine. Celle-ci et l'aire repas sont séparées par l'étagère bleu-clair occupant presque toute la largeur du lieu. Ici une cheminée s'intègre à une partition de même couleur. Dans la cuisine, un îlot vert pistache divise les coins cuisine et repas. Les poutres en bois sont apparentes et vêtues de blanc, comme les murs le long desquels un escalier mène au niveau supérieur.

Este apartamento se distribuye a partir de unas piezas independientes que a la vez ayudan a conseguir una sensación de color en el espacio. Estos volúmenes separados de forma cúbica toman la forma de una chimenea, una librería y una cocina, la cual queda separada del salón mediante una estantería azul que ocupa la mayor parte de la anchura del apartamento. Una isla de color pistacho divide la cocina en las zonas de trabajo y comedor. Algunas vigas de madera se dejaron a la vista y se pintaron en blanco, así como las paredes, junto a una de las cuales circula una escalera que conduce a un nivel superior.

Location: 6ème Arrondissement
Interior Designer: Marie-France de Saint-Félix
Photos: © Olivier Hallot
dsfcrea@aol.com

Rue Desborde-Valmore

In this 340 m² triplex with numerous terraces, the architect decided to eliminate a floor to create an open volume that extends itself towards the roof and favors the entry of natural light. Marie-France de Saint-Félix then introduced a fixed vertical window to unify top and bottom. On the ground floor, the living room opens out onto a summer dining terrace. The first floor contains two bedrooms, two marble bathrooms, an Acajou closet and an office desk. On the last level, a magnificent Greek marble bathroom and a sun-bathing terrace surround the master bedroom.

In diesem 340 m² großen dreistöckigen Apartment mit mehreren Terrassen musste der Architekt eine Ebene opfern, um einen offenen Raum bis zum Dach zu gewinnen und dem Tageslicht Eintritt zu gewähren. Später wurde ein vertikales, feststehendes Fenster installiert. In der unteren Etage öffnet sich das Wohnzimmer auf ein sommerliches Terrassen-Esszimmer. In der ersten Etage befinden sich zwei Zimmer, zwei marmorverkleidete Bäder, ein Umkleideraum aus Kaschbaum und ein Schreibtisch. Auf der obersten Ebene umrahmen ein luxuriöses Bad aus griechischem Marmor und eine Sonnenterrasse das Hauptschlafzimmer.

Rue Desborde-Valmore
Marie-France de Saint-Félix

Dans ce triplex de 340 mêtre carrés agrémenté de plusieurs terrasses, l'architecte a du casser entièrement un plancher porteur pour créer un volume d'ouverture, qui s'envole vers le toit et favorise l'entrée de la lumière naturelle. Marie-France de Saint-Félix a ensuite imaginé une verrière fixe verticale. Au rez de chaussée, le salon s'ouvre sur une terrasse salle à manger d'été. Au premier étage, se troubent deux chambre, deux salles de bains en marbre, un dressing en acajou et un bureau. Le dernier niveau s'articule autour de la chambre des parent, avec une superbe salle de bain en marbre grec et une autre grande terrasse aménagée pour les bains de soleils.

En este triplex de 340 m² con varias terrazas, el arquitecto tuvo que eliminar un nivel para crear un volumen abierto, que se extiende ahora hacia el tejado y favorece la entrada de luz natural. Más tarde se concibió un ventanal fijo vertical. En la planta baja, el salón se abre sobre una terraza-comedor de verano. En el primer piso, se encuentran dos habitaciones, dos baños de mármol, un vestidor de acajú y un escritorio. El último nivel se articula alrededor del dormitorio principal, con un magnífico baño de mármol griego y otra terraza dispuesta para tomar el sol.

Location: 7ème Arrondissement
Architect: Guilhem Roustan
Photos: © Patrick Müller
guilhem.roustan@free.fr

Champs de Mars

This 300 m² apartment suited in a building from the 1900's comprises a contemporary distribution of fluid space with a certain classical style. Finished nearly entirely in marble and parquet, the apartment's main feature is a grand living room carefully furnished to keep this sense of spaciousness. A deep red carpet and sofas make the living area more intimate and comfortable, while the other half is dedicated to display the grand black piano. Traditionally framed floor-to-ceiling windows flood this space with natural light and provide ample views of the exterior.

Dieses 300 m² große Apartment in einem Gebäude um 1900 zeigt eine moderne Raumverteilung mit einem gewissen Touch Klassik. Inmitten von Marmor und Parkett richtet sich die Aufmerksamkeit auf einen riesigen, liebevoll eingerichteten Wohnraum, der den Eindruck von Weitläufigkeit nicht beeinträchtigt. Ein dunkelroter Teppich und eine Sofagarnitur verwandeln den Raum in einen intimen und komfortablen Bereich. Den Rest dieses Zimmers beherrscht das Klavier. Die typischen Fenster vom Boden bis zur Decke erfüllen den Raum mit Tageslicht und geben einen attraktiven Blick nach draußen frei.

Champs de Mars
Guilhem Roustan

Ce 300 m² d'un immeuble 1900 présente une distribution très contemporaine de l'espace avec une touche au classicisme certain. Fini essentiellement en marbre et parquet, cet intérieur est caractérisé par un somptueux séjour, meublé avec amour, pour respecter la sensation d'espace. Un tapis au rouge obscur et un jeu de sofas communiquent une intimité et un confort réels à cette pièce. Un piano occupe le reste de ce lieu. Des fenêtres au design traditionnel, du sol au plafond, inondent l'espace de lumière naturelle et offrent de charmantes vues sur l'extérieur.

Este apartamento de 300 m² situado en un edificio de 1900 presenta una contemporánea distribución de espacio adornada de un cierto estilo clásico. Acabado casi por completo en mármol y parqué, la característica principal del interior radica en una enorme sala de estar amueblada cuidadosamente para respetar la sensación de espacio. Una alfombra en rojo oscuro y un juego de sofás convierten la sala en una zona íntima y confortable. El resto de esta estancia se dedica al piano. Unas ventanas de diseño tradicional que se levantan de suelo a techo llenan el espacio de luz natural y permiten disfrutar de unas bonitas vistas del exterior.

Location: 9ème Arrondissement
Architect: Piret Johanson
Photos: © Olivier Hallot
pirethallot@aol.com

Near Bois de Boulogne

In her Parisian apartment, its creator Piret Johanson found inspiration in Japan, a country that cultivates a balance between fullness and void. She chose furniture with pure lines combined with a palette of relaxing colors that range from neutral to chocolate. To gain space, a 14 meter hallway that distributed the four bedrooms was eliminated, making an 80 m² living room possible. In the dining room, she designed an unusually long table with benches. Apart from industrial shelves in the kitchen, a central island in the kitchen contains the stove, faucets and kitchen appliances.

Piret Johanson hat sich bei ihrem Pariser Apartment von Japan inspirieren lassen, einem Land, das das Gleichgewicht zwischen Fülle und Leere kultiviert. Es wurde ein Mobiliar reiner Linien in Verbindung mit entspannenden Farbtönen zwischen natur- und schokoladenfarben ausgewählt. Um Raum zu gewinnen, entfernte man den 14 Meter langen Gang, an denen sich die vier kleinen Zimmer aufreihten. Dadurch entstand ein 80 m² großes Wohnzimmer und ein Esszimmer mit Tisch und Bänken in wenig üblichen Maßen. In der Küche steht, abgesehen von den Industrieregalen, ein zentral angeordneter Arbeitstisch mit Kochplatten, Töpfen und Küchenutensilien.

Near Bois de Boulogne
Piret Johanson

Dans son appartement parisien la créatrice Piret Johanson a puisé son inspiration de japon, un pays qui cultive l'équilibre entre le plein et le vide. Elle a choisi des meubles aux lignes pures alliés à une palette de couleurs relaxantes allant de l'écru au chocolat. Pour gagner de l'espace, elle a supprimé un couloir de 14 mètres de long qui distribuait les quatre petites pièces du logement. Cela lui a permis de réaliser un salon de 80 mètres carrés. Pour la salle à manger, elle a dessiné une table et des bancs d'une longueur inhabituelle. Dans la cuisine elle a imaginé, à partir d'étagères industrielles, un plan de travail central où sont rassemblés les plaques de cuisson, les éviers et la batterie de casseroles.

En su apartamento parisiense la creadora Piret Johanson se ha inspirado en Japón, un país que cultiva el equilibrio entre lo lleno y lo vacío. Se han elegido muebles de líneas puras combi-nados con una paleta de colores relajantes del crudo al chocolate. Para ganar espacio, se ha suprimido un pasillo de 14 metros de largo que distribuía las cuatro habitaciones pequeñas. Esto ha permitido un salón de 80 m² y un comedor con una mesa y bancos de medida poco habitual. En la cocina, a partir de estanterías industriales, se sitúa una mesa de trabajo central donde se agrupan las placas de cocina y los utensilios de cocina.

Location: 2ème Arrondissement
Architect: Sylvie Chirat
Photos: © Luc Boegly
Tel: + 33 1 4476 09 09

Black, White and Wood

This 95 m² apartment is situated within an industrial building and occupies two of its floors. White walls, wood panelling and lustrous black floors set the stage for a subtle blend of color and furniture that distribute themselves throughout the different areas. The living and dining room form an L-shaped space, a made-to-measure dining table occupying it length. A black and white checkered pattern is repeated in several places, most notably in the kitchen, creating a dramatic effect. In the living area, a large bookcase and a voluminous red chair are the main focal points. Straight and curved lines combine with the curious color combination in this distinguished architect's apartment.

Ein 95 m² großes Apartment in einem alten Industriegebäude bietet eine kuriose Mischung von Materialien und Mobiliar: weiße Wände, Holzpaneele und schwarzglänzende Fußböden. Im L-förmigen Wohn/Esszimmer spielt der maßgeschreinerte Tisch die Hauptrolle. Eine Farbpalette von Weiß und Schwarz wiederholt sich in den Innenräumen und verleiht besonders der Küche ein dramatisches Flair. Das Wohnzimmer wirkt durch das große Bücherregal und einen voluminösen roten Sessel. Die Sequenz von geraden Linien und Bögen sowie die erstaunlichen Farbkombinationen wurde dem Geschmack des Architekten angepasst.

Black, White and Wood
Sylvie Chirat

Un ancien immeuble industriel héberge ce 95 m² occupant deux de ses étages. Il affiche un curieux mélange de matériaux et de mobilier contre des murs blancs, des panneaux de bois et des sols au noir brillant se répétant entre les aires diverses. Une table sur mesure occupe la partie principale du salon-salle à manger en L. Une palette en blanc et noir se répète dans l'ensemble des intérieurs, surtout dans la cuisine, y créant un effet théâtral. Une grande bibliothèque et une belle chaise rouge dominent le salon. Droites et courbes se marient en une étrange association de couleurs dans un appartement au goût d'un architecte.

Este apartamento de 95 m² está situado en un antiguo edificio industrial y ocupa dos de sus pisos. Muestra una curiosa mezcla de materiales y mobiliario, con paredes blancas, paneles de madera y lustrosos suelos negros que se repiten en las distintas áreas. En un salón-comedor con forma de L, una mesa hecha a medida ocupa la parte principal. Una paleta de colores en blanco y negro se repite en el conjunto de los interiores, aunque más notablemente en la cocina, donde consigue un efecto dramático. En el salón, una gran librería y una voluminosa silla roja son los elementos principales. Una secuencia de líneas rectas y curvas se conjuga con una curiosa combinación de colores en este apartamento diseñado al gusto de un arquitecto.

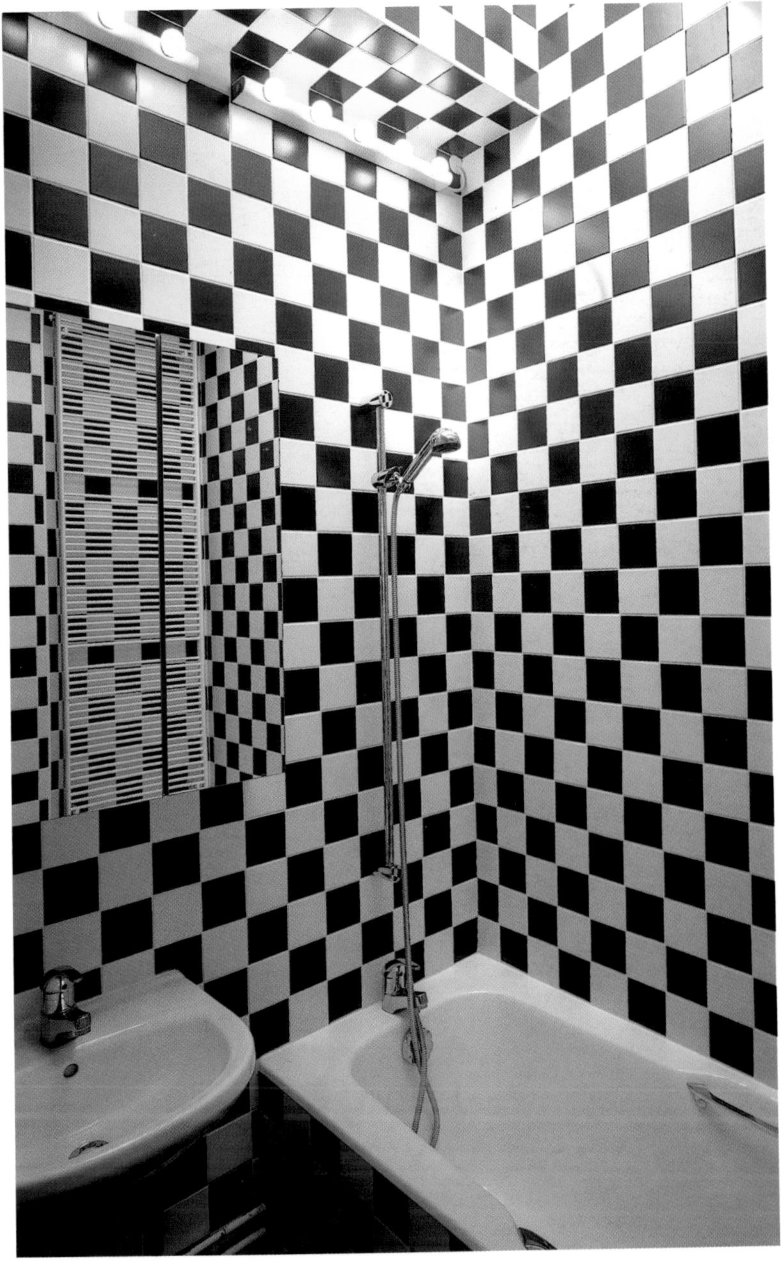

Location: 6ème Arrondissement
Architect: Felice Fanuele
Photos: © Olivier Hallot
fanuele.architecte@wanadoo.fr

Space in Suspense

In a building designed by the architect Henri Sauvage, Felice Fanuele employed a great ingenuity in remodeling this 330 m² twelve-bedroom apartment. The decision to "empty the volume" was unanimous, and so all partitions were eliminated. The front door opens out to an oblique corridor that leads to the living room, offering a welcome surprise: the eye wanders to far-reaching corners of a succession of large open space delineated by shelved partitions. A small living room gives way the TV-Hi-Fi area, then to the dining room, and finally the kitchen. At the other end of the apartment, in the night zone, the ambience is softer and warmer. The sheet metal wall also marks the course from one zone to another and it is at the same time the heart and spine of this apartment's structure.

In einem Gebäude des Architekten Henri Sauvage vom Anfang des Jahrhunderts, hat Felice Fanuele ihren kreativen Geist entfaltet und diese 330 m² und 12 Zimmer umfassende Wohnung umgebaut. Die Eingangstür führt auf einen langen Gang mit schräger Wand zum Wohnzimmer. Dort wandert der Blick über offene, von Wandregalen begrenzte Bereiche zu fernliegenden Ecken. Nach einem kleinen Salon folgt der TV- und Musikraum und danach Esszimmer und Küche. Am anderen Ende, dem Nachtbereich, ist die Atmosphäre wärmer. Die Wand aus Stahlblech mit Edelrost ist Übergang von einem Bereich in den anderen und gleichzeitig das Herz der Wohnung.

Space in Suspense
Felice Fanuele

Dans un immeuble de l'architecte Henri Sauvage, Felice Fanuele a déployé des trésors d'ingéniosité pour remodeler cet appartement de 330 m², qui comptait douze pièces. Toutes les cloisons ont été éliminées. La porte d'entrée s'ouvre sur une longue paroi oblique qui mène vers le salon, tout en le dissimulant. Au seuil du séjour, surprise... Le regard s'envole pour s'arrêter après une enfilade de zones ouvertes délimitées par des parios-rangements. On traverse un autre petit salon, l'espace tv/hifi, la salle à manger puis la cuisine. A l'autre extrémité de l'appartment le climat est plus doux pour la partie nuit. La pario en tôle patinée marque le passage d'un domaine à l'autre. Elle est à la fois le coeur et la colonne vertébrale de la maison.

En un edificio del arquitecto de principios de siglo Henri Sauvage, Felice Fanuele ha desplegado su ingenio para remodelar este apartamento de 330 m² que tenía doce habitaciones. La puerta de entrada da a una larga pared oblicua que conduce al salón. Una vez allí, la mirada se detiene decenas de metros más lejos, después de una sucesión de zonas abiertas delimitadas por paredes-estanterías: otro pequeño salón, el espacio de televisión y música, el comedor y la cocina. En el otro extremo del apartamento, la zona de noche, el ambiente es más cálido. La pared de chapa patinada marca el paso de una zona a otra y, como si fuera una escultura, es a la vez el corazón y la columna vertebral del interior.

Location: 13ème Arrondissement
Architect: Alain Salomon
Photos: © Alain Salomon
apsalomon@wanadoo.fr

Rue de Croulebarbe

A simple structure and a regular E-shape layout define the setting of this apartment, which manages to conjure up, in a confined but superbly exploited space, the essence of an open but peaceful home. The sobriety of the materials, combined with natural light, turns an apartment seemingly governed by functional considerations into an attractive and relaxing space. The various areas are efficiently connected and astutely organized to conveniently provide freedom of movement; the decoration incorporates modern designs but focuses on practicality and comfort over and above passing fashions. The project devised by the architect Alain Salomon makes no concessions to the latest trends; its ruling criteria are good taste and meticulousness.

Eine einfache Struktur und eine Grundfläche in E-Form bilden den Hintergrund dieses Apartments, das auf engem Raum zu einer offenen und ruhigen Wohnung gestaltet wird. Die zurückhaltende Verwendung von Materialien in einer vom Tageslicht durchfluteten Umgebung verwandelt die ursprünglich reine Funktionalität in einen friedvollen und attraktiven Raum. Die Räumlichkeiten sind unkompliziert miteinander verbunden und die praktisch orientierte und gleichzeitig komfortable Dekoration macht keine Konzessionen an vorübergehende Modetendenzen. Das Projekt des Architekten Alain Salomon wird bestimmt von Stilreinheit und Formenstrenge.

Rue de Croulebarbe
Alain Salomon

Une structure simple et un niveau régulier en E sont la toile de fond de cet appartement qui sait recréer avec peu d'espace, bien exploité, l'essence d'une maison ouverte et paisible. La sobriété des matériaux confrontée à la lumière métamorphosent un endroit fonctionnel en principe en un lieu serein et séduisant. Les espaces, communiquant parfaitement et distribués sensément, libèrent le mouvement et la décoration, respectant l'esthétique contemporaine, cherche le côté pratique et le confort, sans céder à la mode éphémère. Signé par l'architecte Alain Salomon, le projet va au-delà des tendances, guidé par le bon sens et la rigueur.

Una sencilla estructura y una planta regular en forma de E son el telón de fondo de este apartamento que consigue recrear en pocos metros muy bien aprovechados la esencia de una vivienda abierta y tranquila. El sobrio empleo de los materiales bañados por la luz natural transforma lo que en un principio es simple funcionalidad en un ambiente sosegado y atractivo. Las estancias, perfectamente comunicadas y organizadas con acierto, permiten una cómoda libertad de movimientos, y la decoración, que no prescinde de la estética contemporánea, busca una practicidad y un confort que jamás se somete ni hace concesiones a la moda pasajera. El proyecto, firmado por el arquitecto Alain Salomon, va más allá de las tendencias y se rige por el buen criterio y el rigor.

Location: 9ème Arrondissement
Architect: Alain Salomon
Photos: © Alain Salomon, Gaston Bergeret
apsalomon@wanadoo.fr

Rue Milton

When the architect Alain Salomon drew up the plans for this Paris apartment his main aim was to create a continuous, uniform space in which all the different areas were integrated yet at the same time separated according to their function. Faced with an irregular layout dominated by straight lines, Salomon came up with the ingenious and practical solution of dividing off some areas with colored panels –a ruse which also preserves the privacy of the bedroom adjoining the living room– and putting the shower area in a module in the middle of the space in front of the kitchen. These interventions provide effective answers to the practical problems posed by the apartment while also taking full advantage of the space available.

Der Architekt Alain Salomon konzipierte dieses Pariser Apartment als einen einheitlichen und zusammenhängenden Raum mit Bereichen, die gleichzeitig darin integriert aber doch voneinander getrennt sind. Angesichts einer Fläche mit geraden aber etwas unregelmäßigen Linien entschied er sich für die geniale und praktische Lösung, einige Bereiche mit farbigen Paneelen abzuteilen – um Neugierigen den Blick ins Schlafzimmer zu versperren – oder die Dusche in ein geometrisches Modul vor der Küche unterzubringen. So werden wirkungsvoll alle praktischen Probleme der Wohnung gelöst und gleichzeitig die verfügbare Fläche optimal genutzt.

Rue Milton
Alain Salomon

En projetant cet appartement, l'architecte Alain Salomon tendait à créer un espace uni et continu où les surfaces s'intégreraient en restant séparées, selon leur fonction. Sur un étage de lignes droites mais irrégulier, le parti fut pris de l'ingéniosité et de la pratique : diviser des zones avec des cloisons colorées, préservant ici des curieux la chambre jouxtant le salon de la vue, ou intégrant le coin douche (séparé du bain) en un volume géométrique, au centre de l'espace restant devant la cuisine. Ainsi sont résolues efficacement les considérations pratiques de l'habitation, tout en profitant pleinement des dimensions disponibles.

Obtener un espacio uniforme y continuo en el que las diferentes áreas estuvieran integradas a la vez que separadas según su funcionalidad fue una de las premisas que siguió el arquitecto Alain Salomon al proyectar este apartamento parisiense. Ante una planta de líneas rectas y algo irregular, se optó por emplear la ingeniosa y práctica solución de dividir algunas áreas con paneles de color –recurso que permite preservar de la mirada de curiosos el dormitorio situado junto al salón– o integrar la zona de la ducha en un volumen geométrico en medio del área que queda ante la cocina. Se logra así resolver de una manera eficaz todas las consideraciones prácticas de la vivienda al mismo tiempo que se aprovecha al máximo el espacio existente.

Location: Paris
Architect: Christophe Pillet
Photos: © Jean François Jaussaud
Fax: +33 1 4806 7832

Luminous Continuity

This project is located in a former office space which was converted into a residence. Thanks to the tall windows there is an abundance of natural light, which compensates for the limited interior surface area. Hallways and partitions were avoided, except in the bathroom where a sliding door divides it from the bedroom to provide privacy. The kitchen, situated near the entrance, incorporates two small modules in one of its lateral walls. The two façades contain no installations, allowing for the large windows to remain free of structural restraints.

Das Projekt liegt in einem alten Bürogebäude, das später für Wohnungen umgebaut wurde. Dank der hohen Fenster flutet reichlich natürliches Licht herein und vergrößert so den begrenzten Innenraum. Gänge und Raumunterteilungen wurden vermieden mit Ausnahme des Bades und einer Schiebetür zur Abtrennung des Schlafzimmers. In der Küche gegenüber dem Eingang nimmt eine Seitenwand zwei Module auf. Da sich in keiner der beiden Fassaden Installationen befinden, konnten die Glasfenster eingelassen werden ohne durch strukturelle Vorgaben Beeinträchtigungen zu erleiden.

Luminous Continuity
Christophe Pillet

Le projet se situe dans un ancien espace de bureaux réformé en logement. La lumière naturelle abonde par de hautes fenêtres, compensant ainsi la surface intérieure limitée. Couloirs et séparations entre les espaces ont été évités, sauf pour le bain et une porte coulissante séparant et protégeant l'intimité de la chambre. La cuisine, face à l'entrée, comprend deux petits modules dans un mur latéral. Les deux façades n'abritent aucune installation et accueillent ainsi des fenêtres vitrées aucunement limitées par des impératifs structurels.

El proyecto se ubica en un antiguo espacio dedicado a oficinas reconvertido en vivienda. Gracias a unas altas ventanas abunda la luz natural, que ayuda a compensar las limitadas dimensiones de la superficie. Se evitaron pasillos y divisiones entre estancias, excepto para el baño y el dormitorio, en el que una puerta deslizante separa y da privacidad al ambiente. La cocina, situada frente a la entrada, incluye dos pequeños módulos en un muro lateral. Las dos fachadas no contienen ningún tipo de instalación, por lo que pueden albergar las ventanas sin quedar predeterminadas por requisitos estructurales.

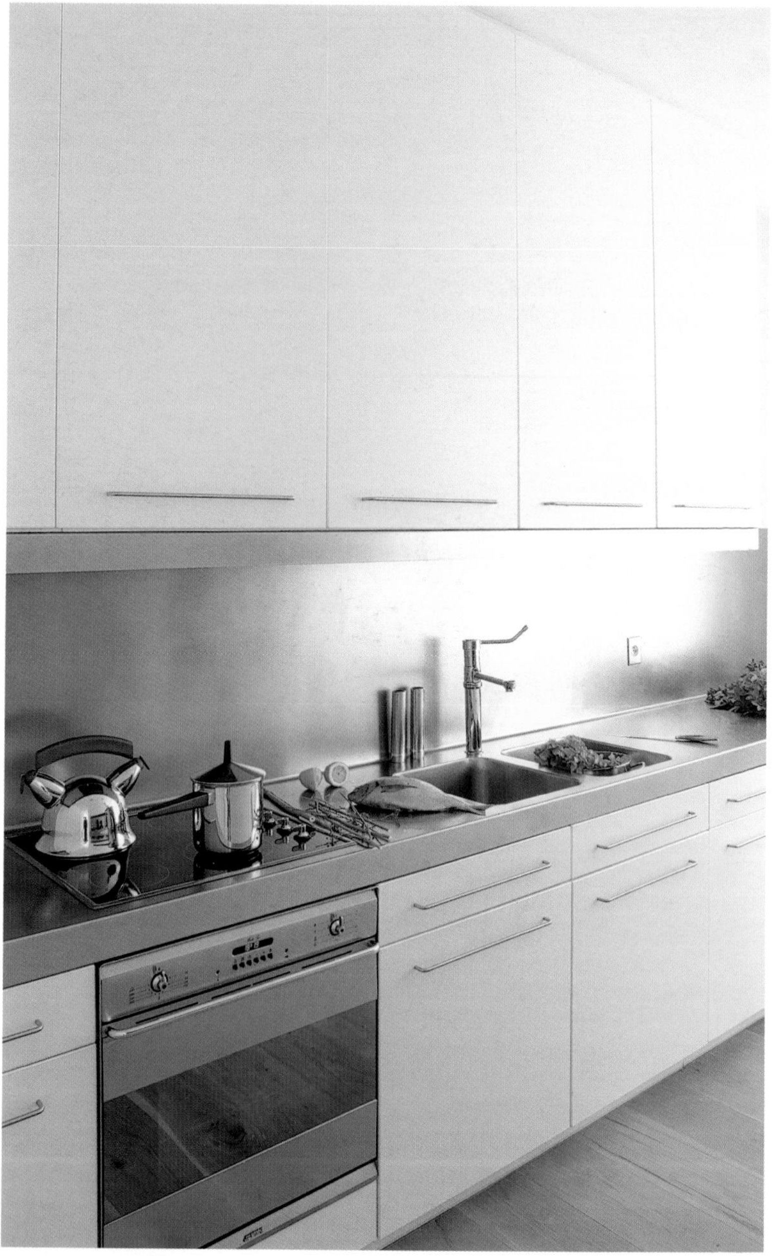

Location: 6ème Arrondisement
Interior Designer: Franziska Kessler (Stylist)
Photos: © Roland Beaufre (Agence Top)
Fax: +33 1 4544 54 20

Café au Lait

The omnipresence of white mingles with neutral tones and natural materials in this soothing and graceful space. A home-away-from-home, Swiss interior designer Franziska Kessler and her husband Daniel have decorated this 78 m² flat as a dwelling that imposes relaxation and contemplation. White surfaces, earth tones, unpolished natural wood and plenty of light make this kind of atmosphere possible. Vintage pieces and an elegant display maintain simplicity and create a space that is simultaneously stylish, contemporary and refined.

Die allgegenwärtige Mischung weißer und neutraler Farbtöne mit natürlichen Materialien ist der auffälligste dekorative Aspekt dieser beeindruckenden Wohnung von nur 78 m². Die Gestaltung haben die Eigentümer, die schweizer Raumausstatterin Franziska Kessler und ihr Ehemann Daniel, selbst übernommen. Obwohl sie mehr Zeit außerhalb als zu Hause verbringen, ist ihnen eine Atmosphäre gelungen, die Entspannung ermöglicht. Weiße Oberflächen, Erdfarben, unbehandeltes Holz und viel Tageslicht führen zu dem gewünschten Effekt. Einige Kunstwerke unterstreichen den einfachen Charakter und schaffen einen stilvollen und eleganten zeitgenössischen Raum.

Café au Lait
Franziska Kessler

L'omniprésence des tons blancs mélangés aux touches neutres et aux matériaux naturels est l'élément primordial de cet espace impressionnant, de seulement 78 m². La décoratrice suisse Franzisca Kessler et son mari Daniel sont les propriétaires et créateurs de cet intérieur. Ils ont su y créer une ambiance relaxante, en dépit d'un rythme de vie qui les en éloigne plus qu'à leur tour. Surfaces blanches, couleurs terre, essences naturelles brutes et généreuse lumière naturelle engendrent l'effet souhaité. Des œuvres anciennes présentées avec élégance entretiennent une simplicité certaine et créent un espace stylé, contemporain et raffiné.

La omnipresencia de mezclas de tonos blancos y neutros con materiales de procedencia natural es el elemento que más resalta en la decoración de esta impactante vivienda de tan solo 78 m². Los propietarios y autores del diseño interior son la decoradora suiza Franziska Kessler y su marido, Daniel, quienes, pese a estar más tiempo fuera de su apartamento que en él, han logrado un ambiente que propicia la relajación. Superficies blancas, colores tierra, maderas naturales sin tratar y una gran cantidad de luz natural consiguen el efecto deseado. La austeridad ornamental se mantiene con la elección de unas piezas de arte como elementos decorativos. El resultado es un espacio con estilo, contemporáneo y refinado.